ACOUSTIC CLASSICS

Led Zeppelin

VOL. 1

© 1995 ALFRED PUBLISHING CO., INC.
All Rights Reserved

ISBN 0 - 89724 - 589 - X

CONTENTS

Key To Notation Symbols

Guitar

Bend   Bend and release   Pre-bend   Pre-bend and release   Quarter step (microtone) bend   Hold bend

Interval bend and release   Unison bend   Bend with fixed tone   Melodic bending with bar   Dip with bar   Dive with bar

Hammer-on   Pull-off   Right hand tap to pull-off   Slide   Pick slide   Arpeggio

Chord shape arpeggiation   Rake   Sweep   Vibrato   Vibrato with bar   Percussive tones (no pitch)

Palm-muting   Harmonics   Artificial harmonics (pick or pinch)   Tremolo picking   Trill

BABE I'M GONNA LEAVE YOU

Words and Music by
ANNE BREDON, JIMMY PAGE
and **ROBERT PLANT**

Moderately slow with halftime feel ♩ = 138
Intro:

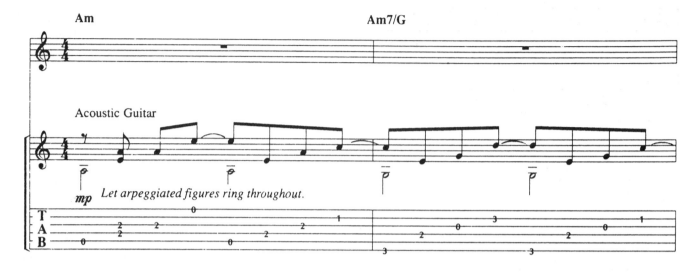

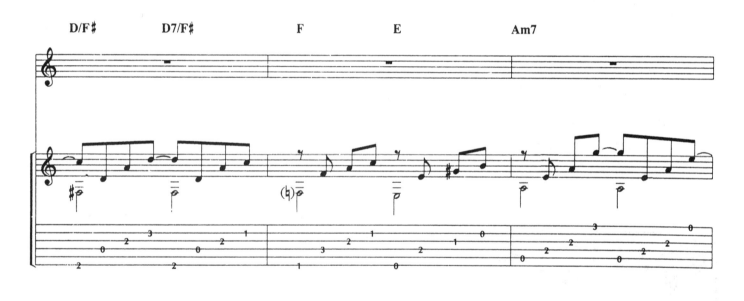

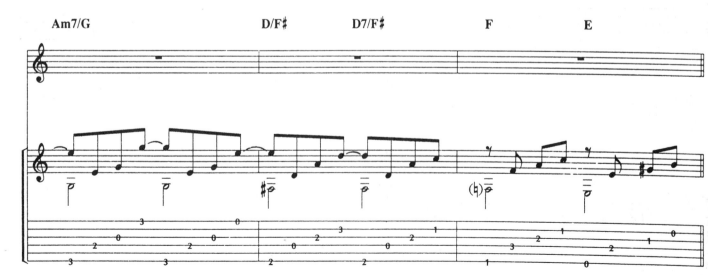

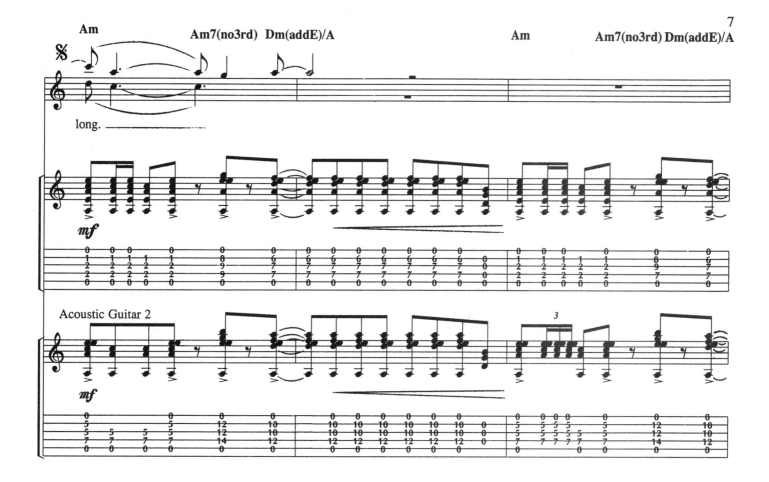

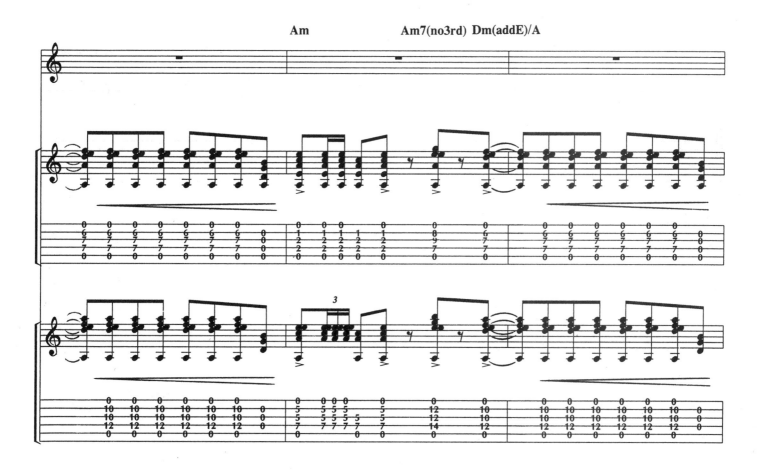

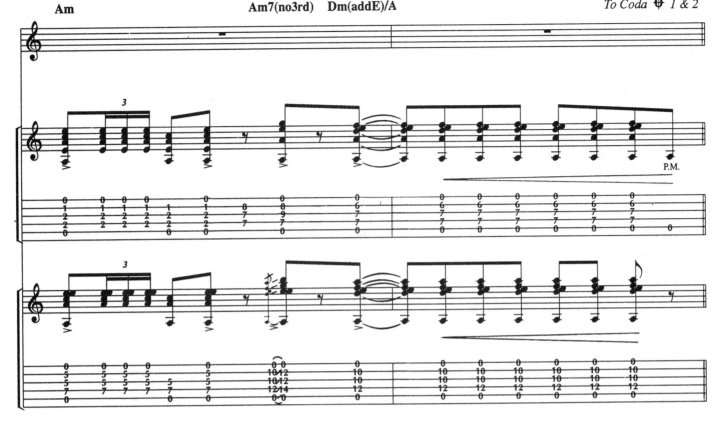

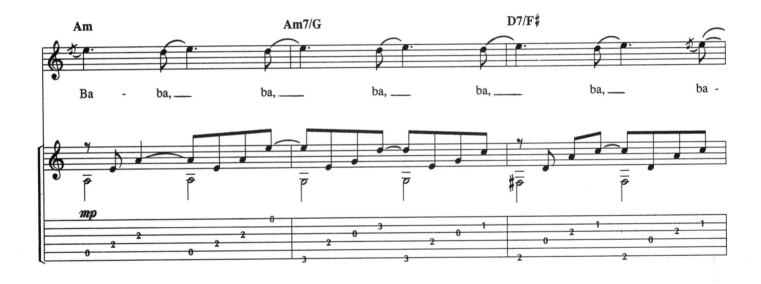

Ba - ba, ___ ba, ___ ba, ___ ba, ___ ba, ___ ba -

by, mmm ba-by I don'twan-na leave ___ you ___

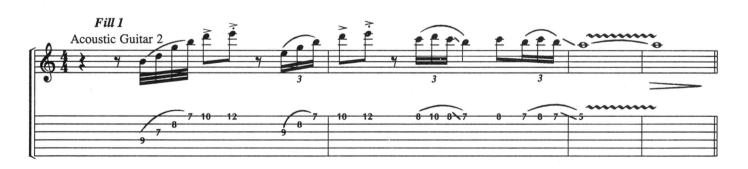

Coda 1

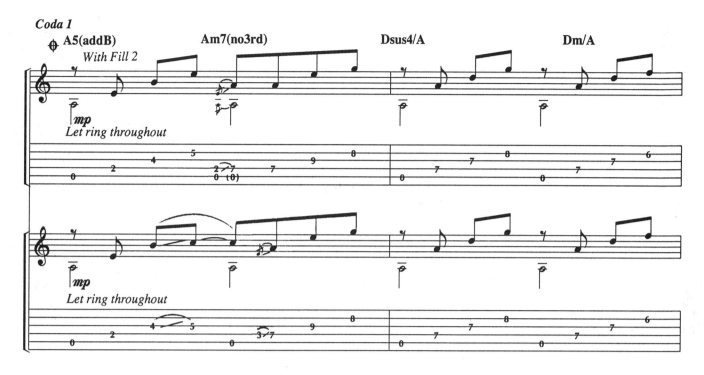

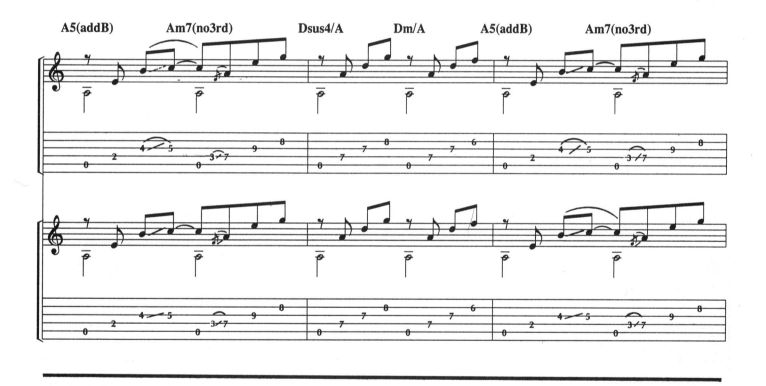

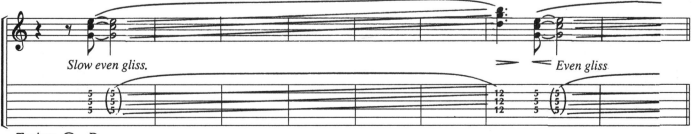

Fill 2
Slide Guitar (*with backwards echo*)

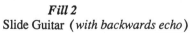

Tuning: ① =D

12

Vocal ad lib. on D.S.

Ba - by, ___ C'mon, Babe!

Acoustic Guitar *With Riff A(4 times) and*
With Fill 4 (16 times)

Electric Guitar

Riff A

Fill 4

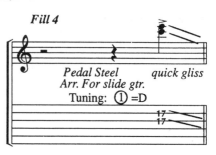

Pedal Steel *quick gliss*
Arr. For slide gtr.
Tuning: ① =D

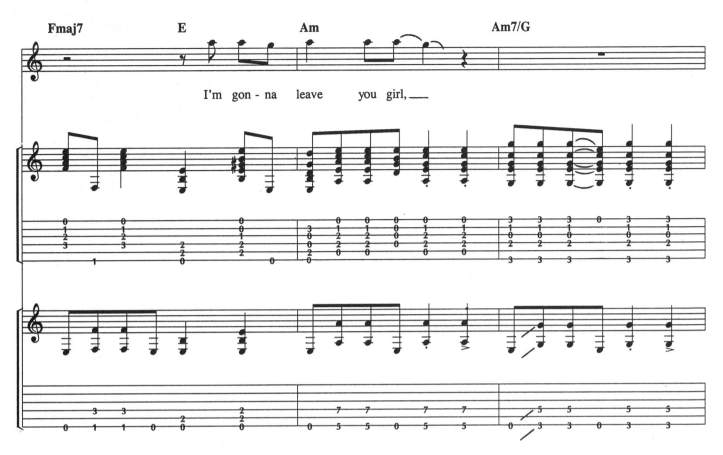

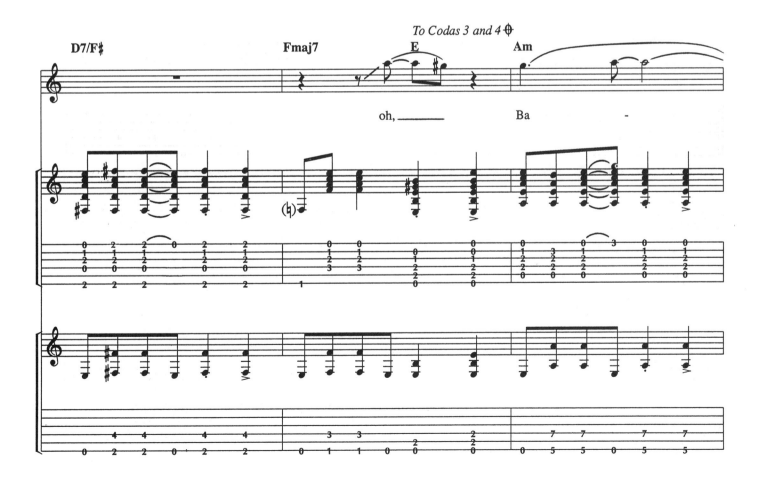

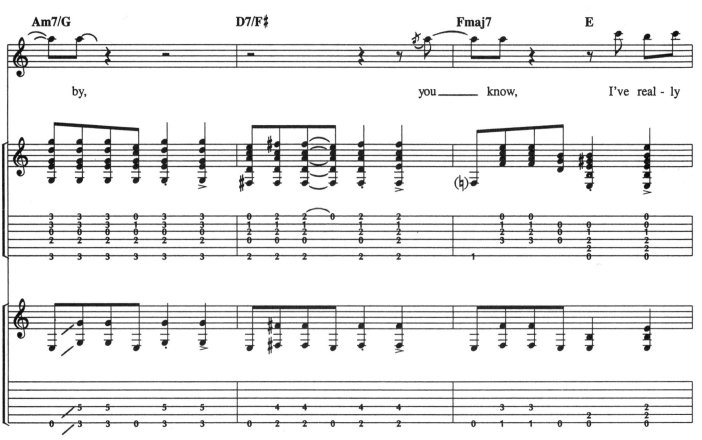

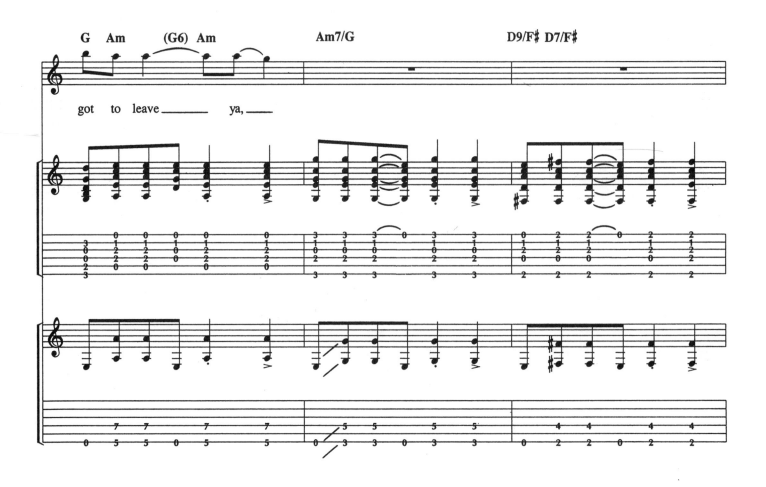

Coda 2

used   to   do. ___

Acoustic Guitar Solo

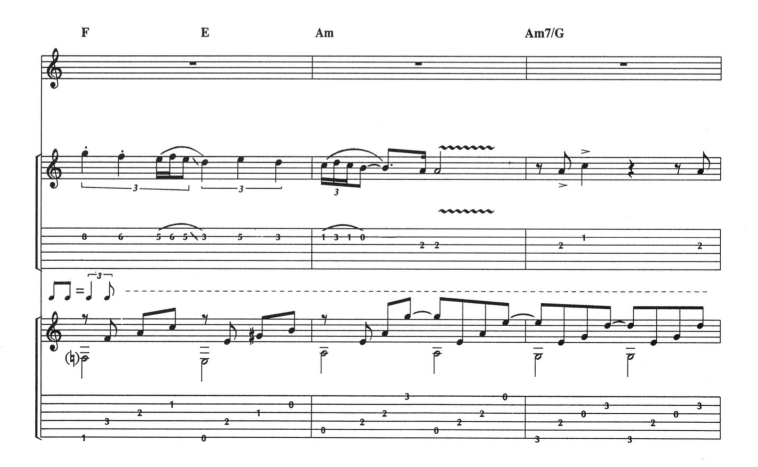

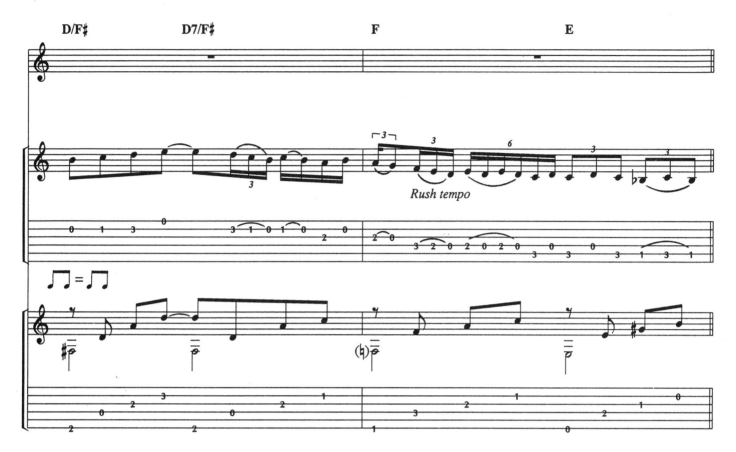

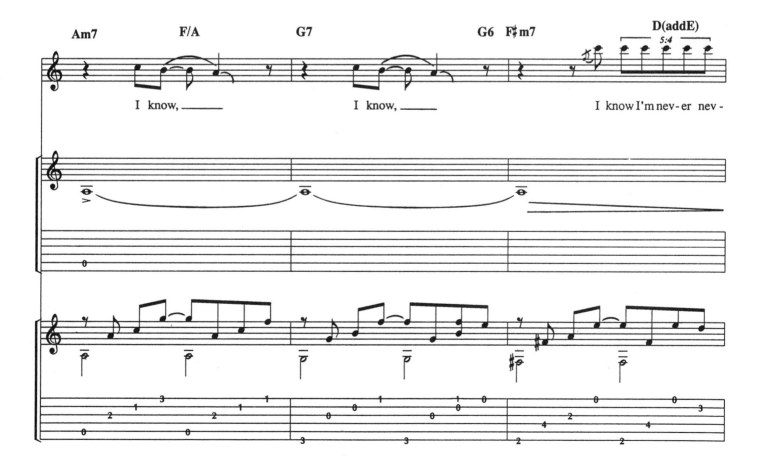

I know, _____   I know, _____   I know I'm nev-er nev-

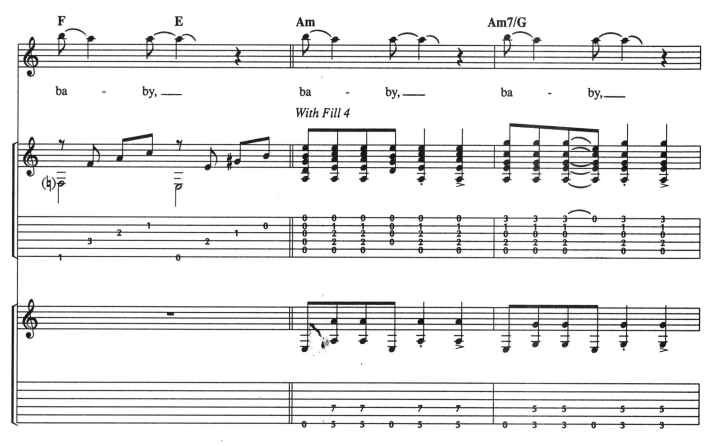

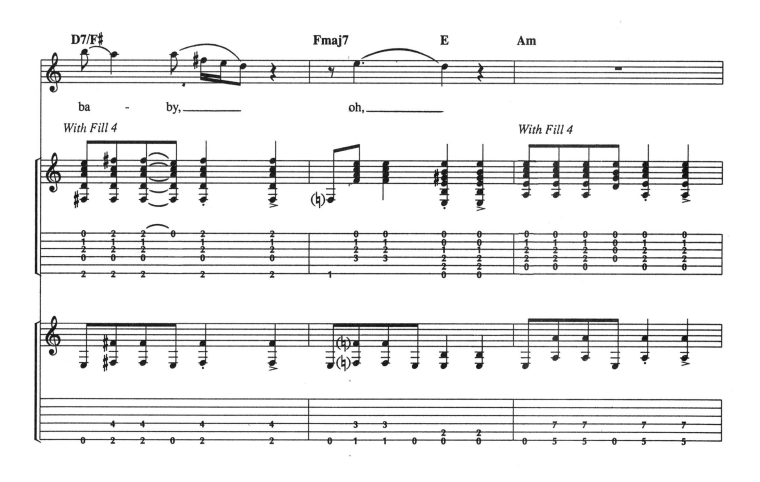

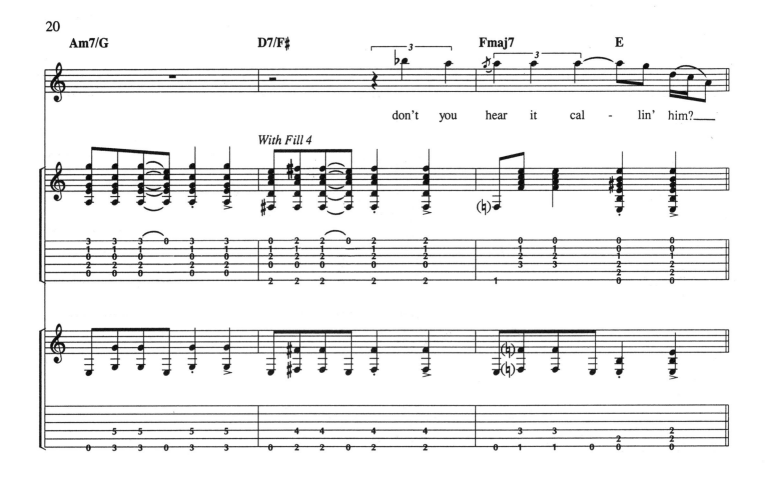

don't you hear it cal - lin' him?____

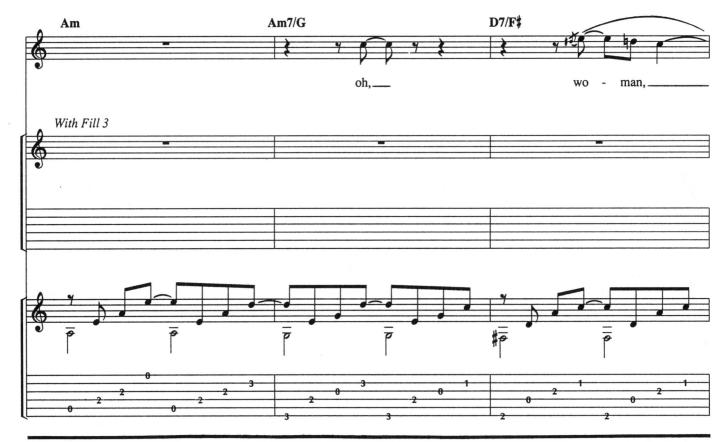

oh,____   wo - man,____

Fill 3

Even gliss.

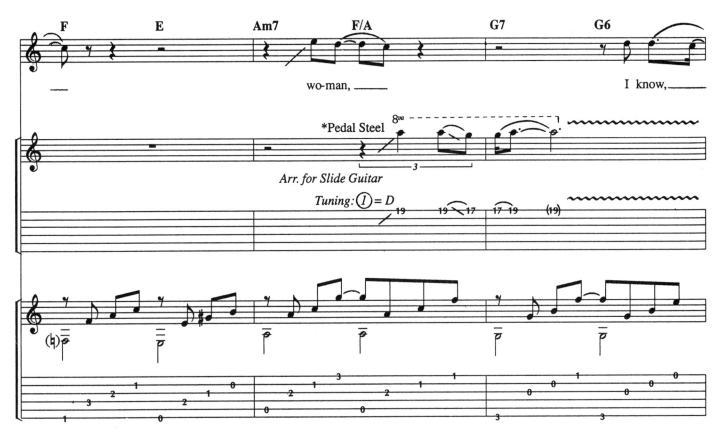

(Alternate fingering)

gain and not know_ that one day ba - by,___ it's real - ly gon-na

D.S.S. 𝄋𝄋 al Coda 3 ⊕

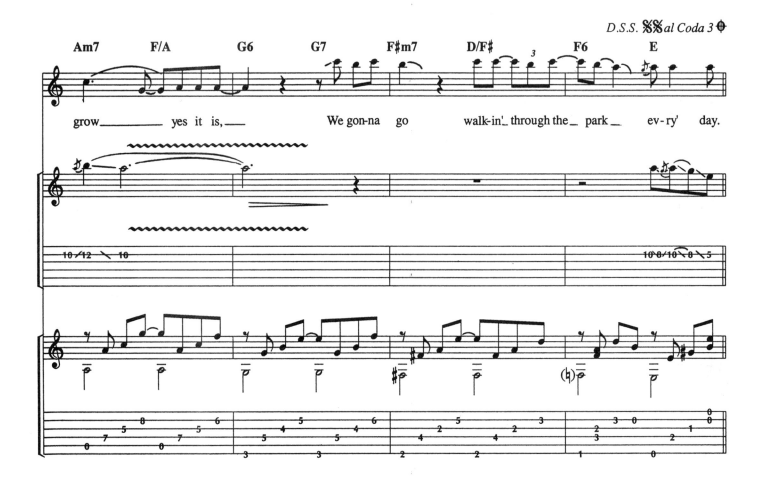

grow_____ yes it is,___ We gon-na go walk-in'_ through the_ park_ ev-ry' day.

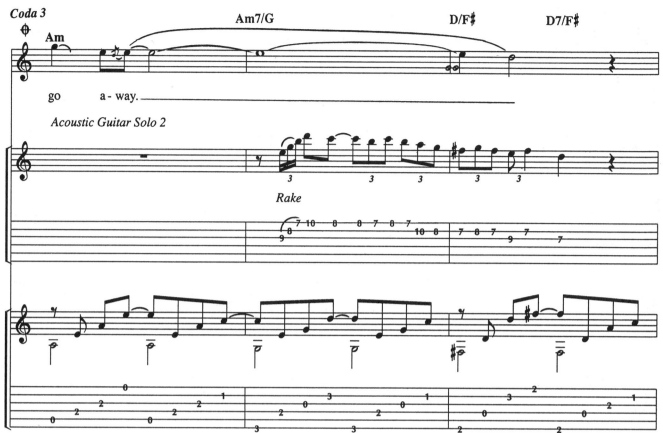

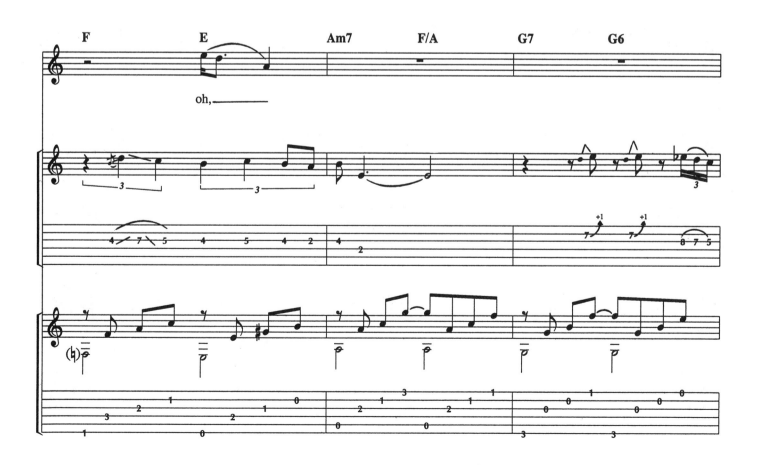

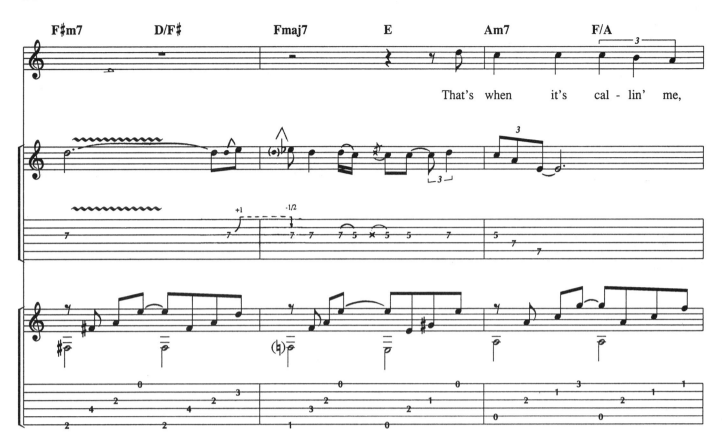

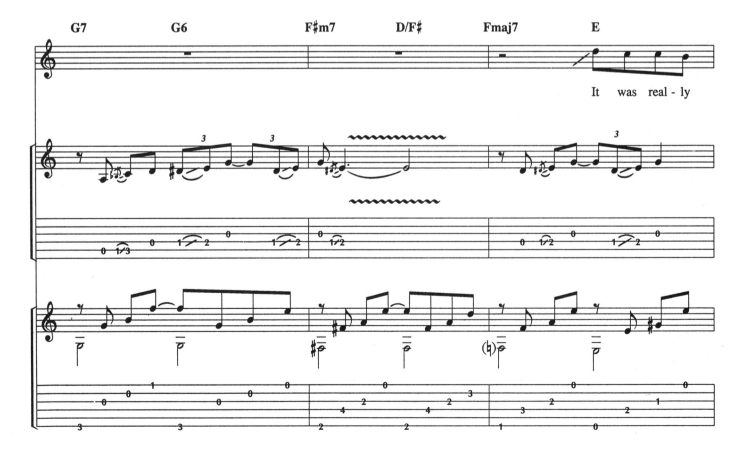

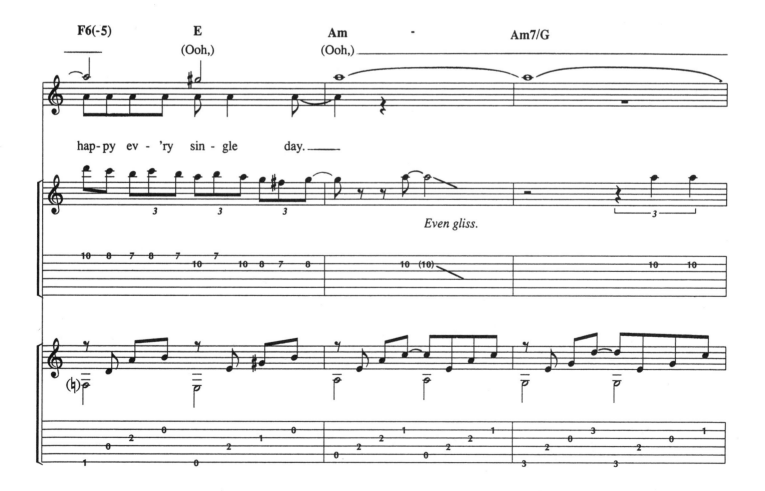

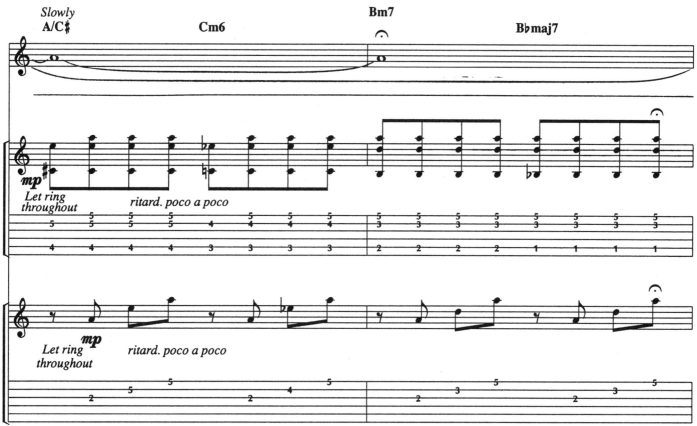

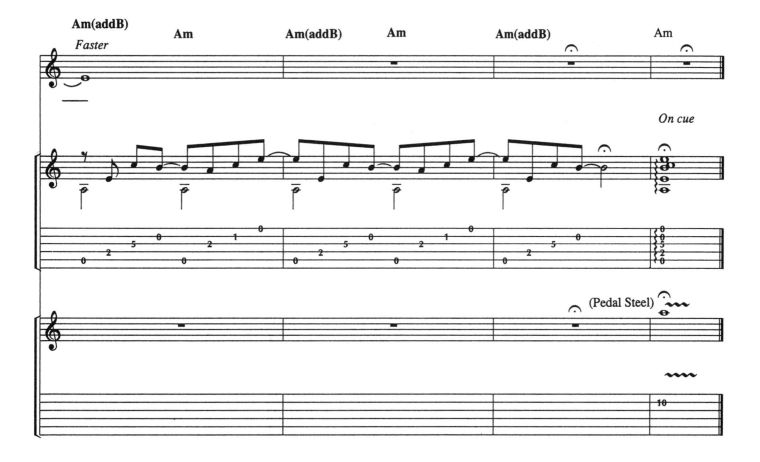

BRON-Y-AUR STOMP

Words and Music by
JIMMY PAGE, ROBERT PLANT
and JOHN PAUL JONES

Moderate Country Folk Dance ♩ = 116

Intro:
Acoustic Guitar * (open F tuning)

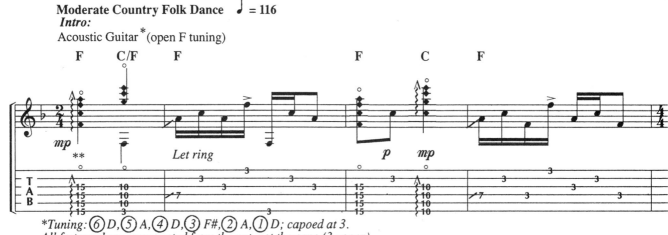

Tuning: ⑥ D, ⑤ A, ④ D, ③ F#, ② A, ① D; capoed at 3.
All fret numbers are counted from the nut, not the capo (3=open).

***Harmonics:** Tilt hand and lightly touch strings with fourth finger at XV.*

(Double time feel)

****Feel it like 4/8 + 2/4; double time: "1-2-3-4" and regular time: "1-2," for four measures, beginning with measure 3, beat 3.*
Also, bar all six strings for all chords, but primarily strum only those strings indicated.

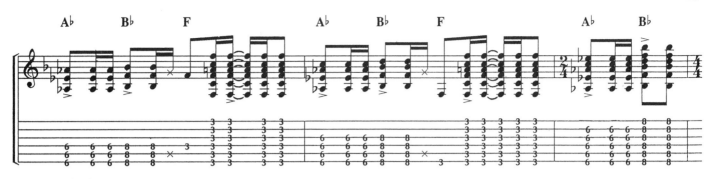

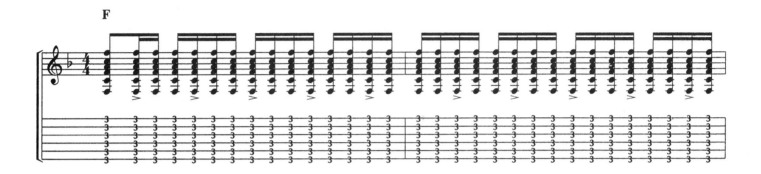

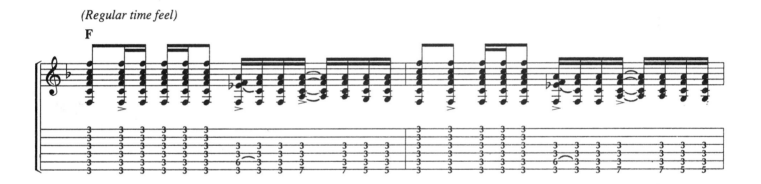

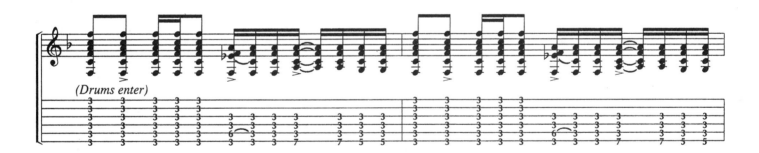

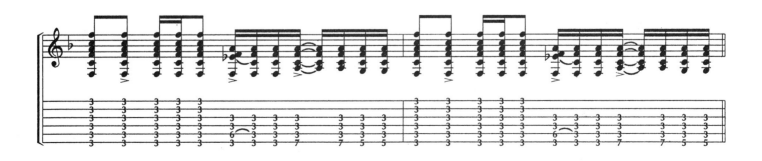

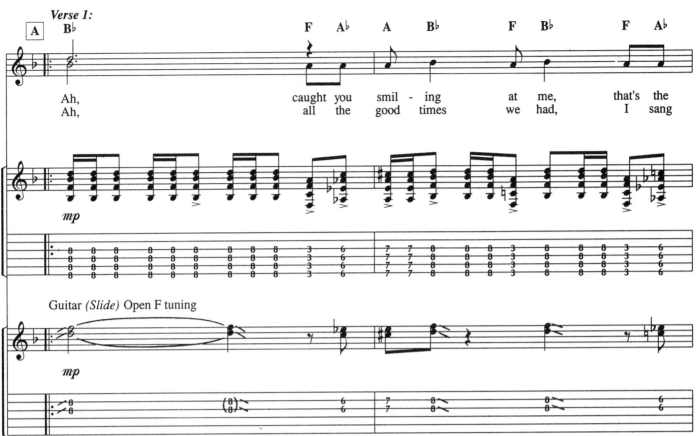

fine.____
fine.____

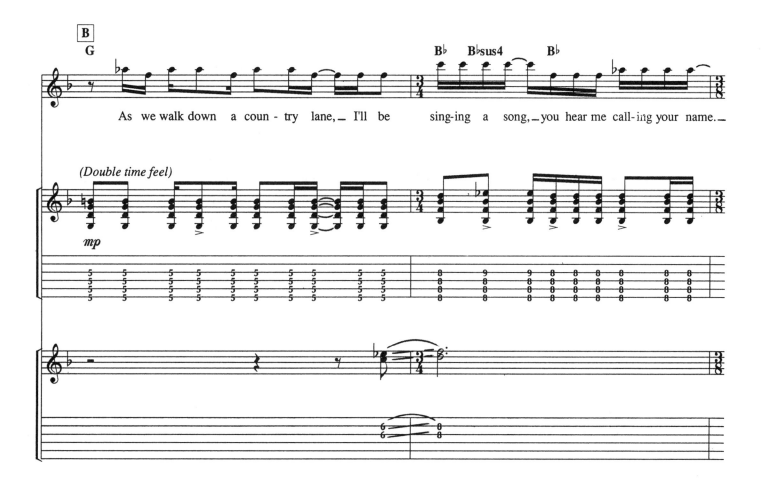

As we walk down a coun-try lane,__ I'll be sing-ing a song,__ you hear me call-ing your name.__

(Double time feel)

Hear the wind whis-per in the trees__ tell-ing Moth-er Na - ture 'bout you and me.

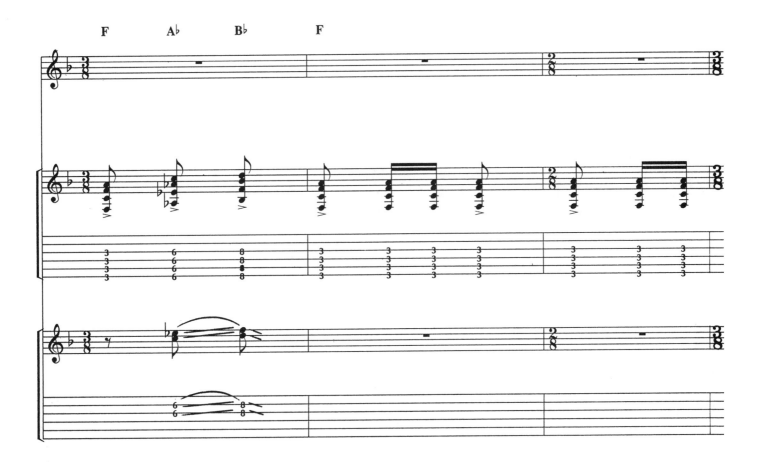

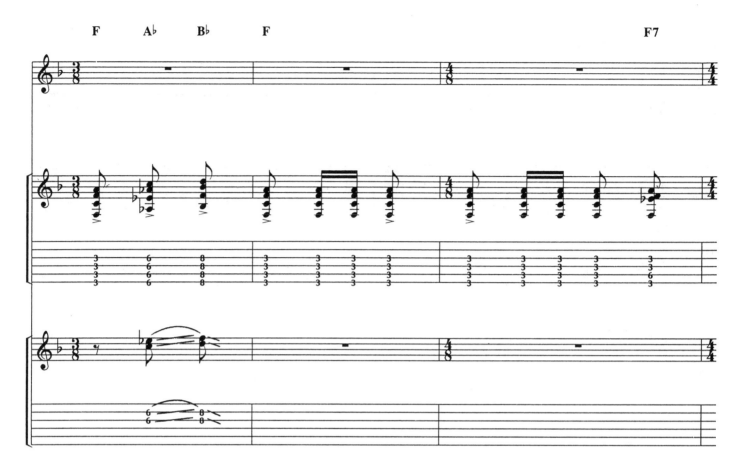

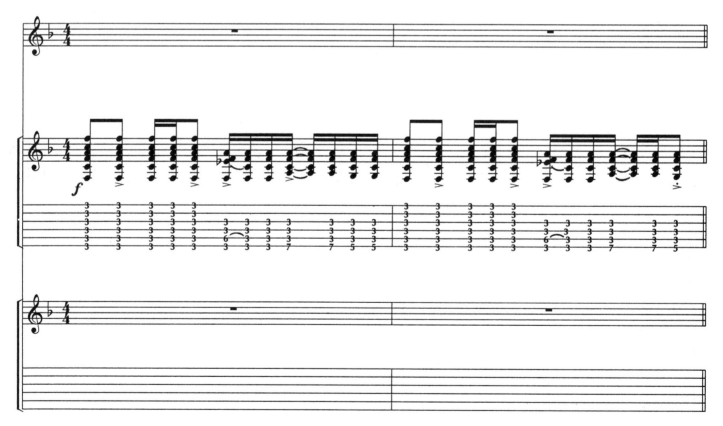

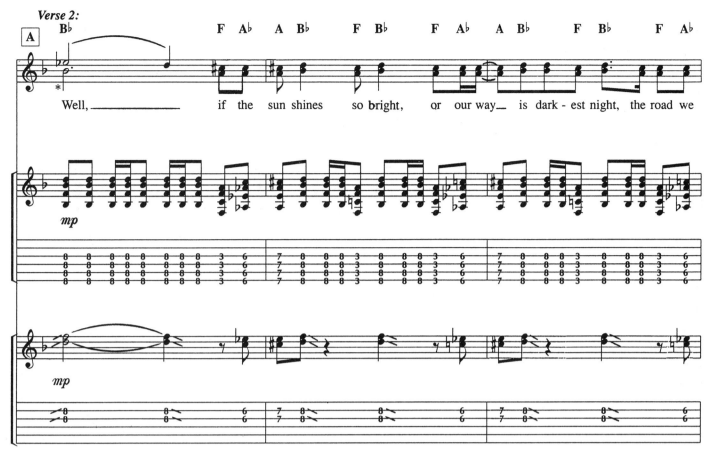

*Lower part is lead vocal throughout.

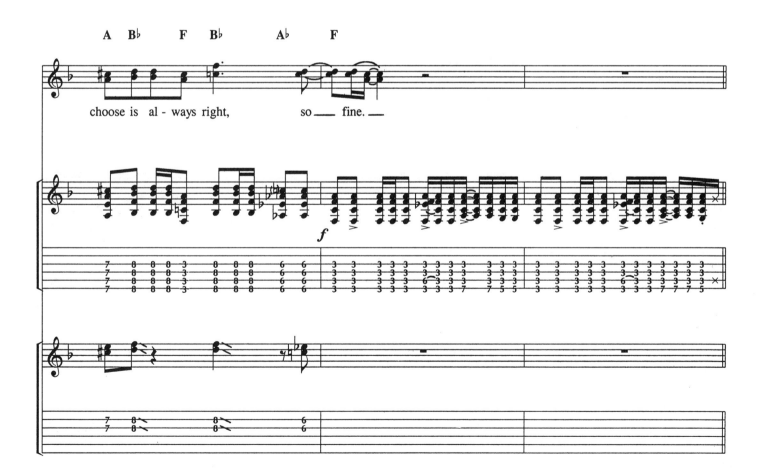

Verse 3:

Ah, can a love be so strong when so man-y loves__ go wrong? Will our

love go on and on, and on,__ and on,__ and on,__ and on?__

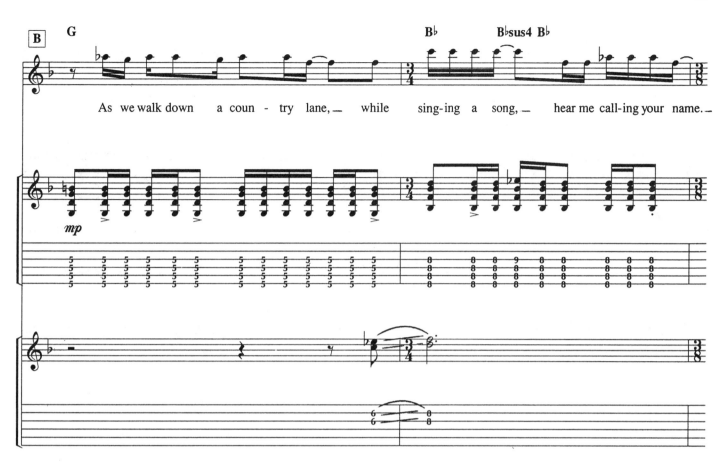

As we walk down a coun - try lane, __ while sing-ing a song, __ hear me call-ing your name. __

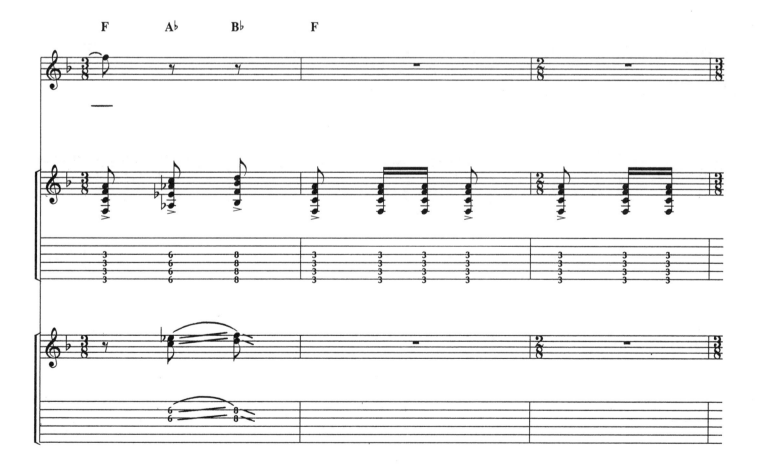

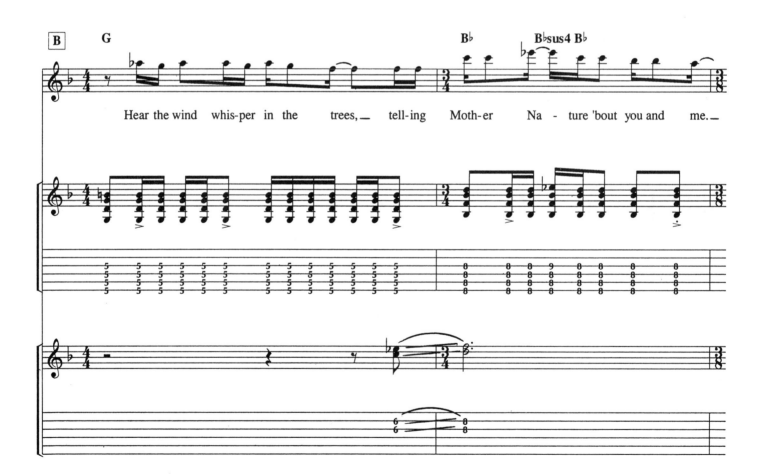

Hear the wind whis-per in the trees, __ tell-ing Moth-er Na - ture 'bout you and me. __

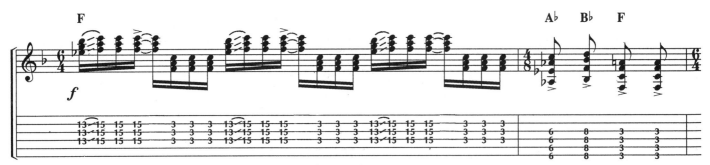

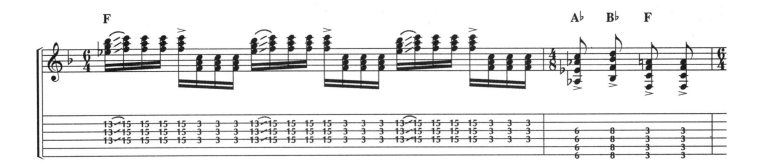

C Verse 4:

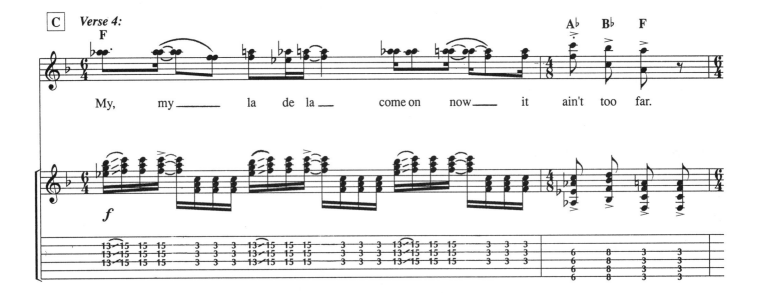

My, my _____ la de la _____ come on now ___ it ain't too far.

Tell your friends _ all a-round the world _ ain't no com-pan - ion like a blue eyed _ merle. _

Harmony *Lead vocal*

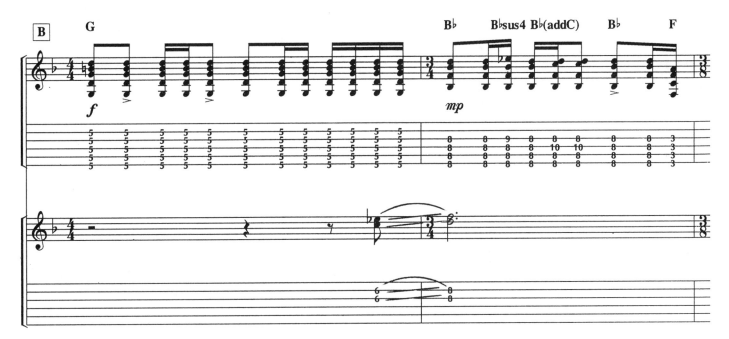

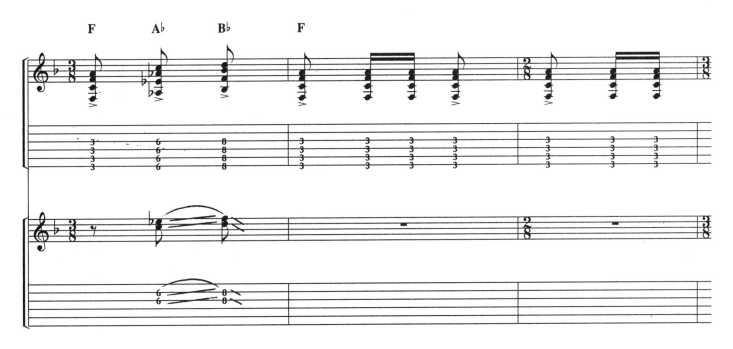

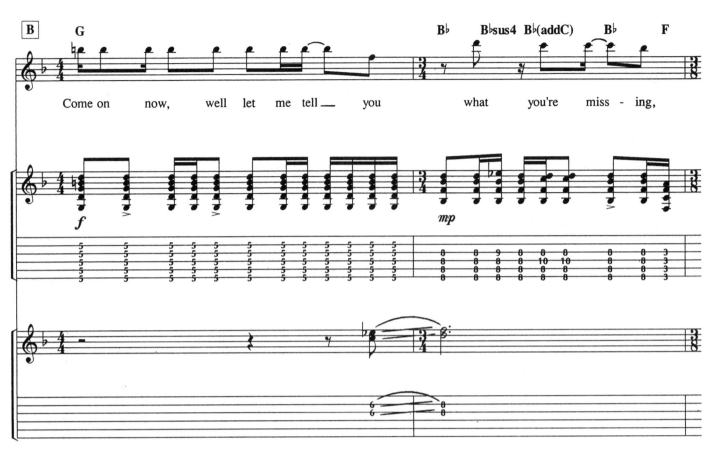

Come on now, well let me tell ___ you what you're miss - ing,

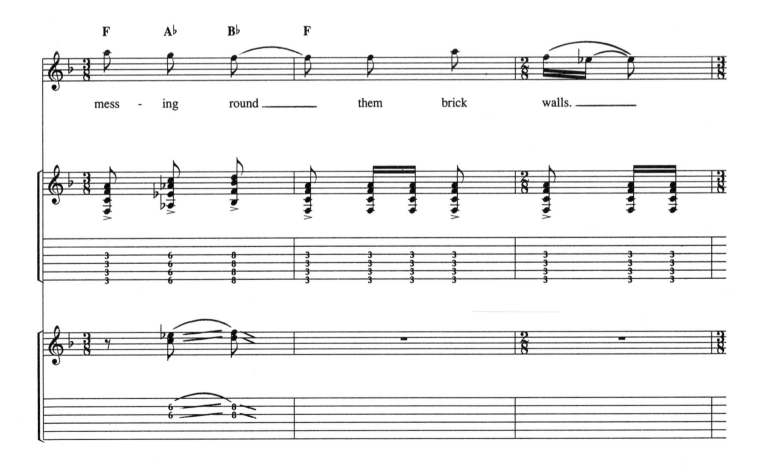

mess - ing round _____ them brick walls. _____

Intro:

44

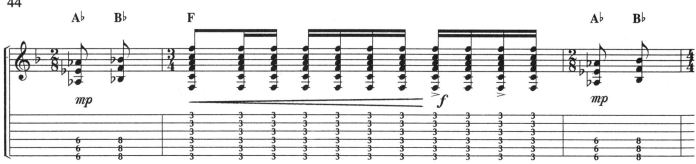

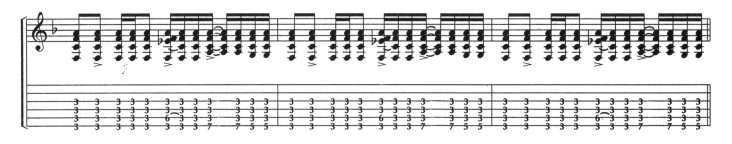

Verse 5:

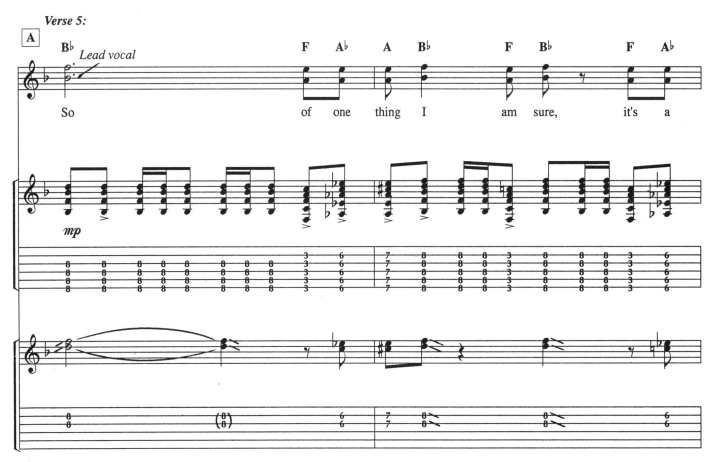

So ... of one thing I am sure, it's a

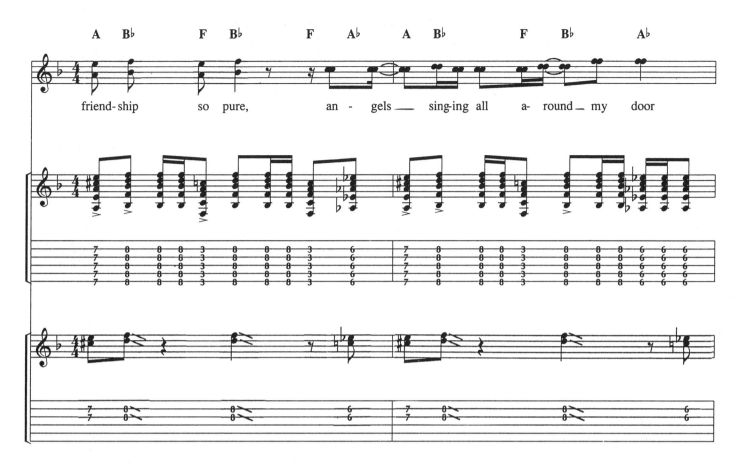

friend-ship so pure, an - gels —— sing-ing all a- round —— my door

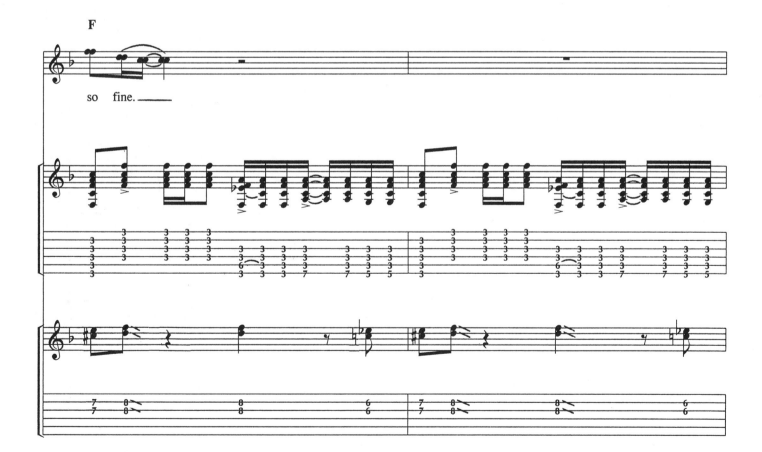

so fine. ——

fine.

When you're old and your eyes are dim there ain't no old shep gon-na happen a -

gain.

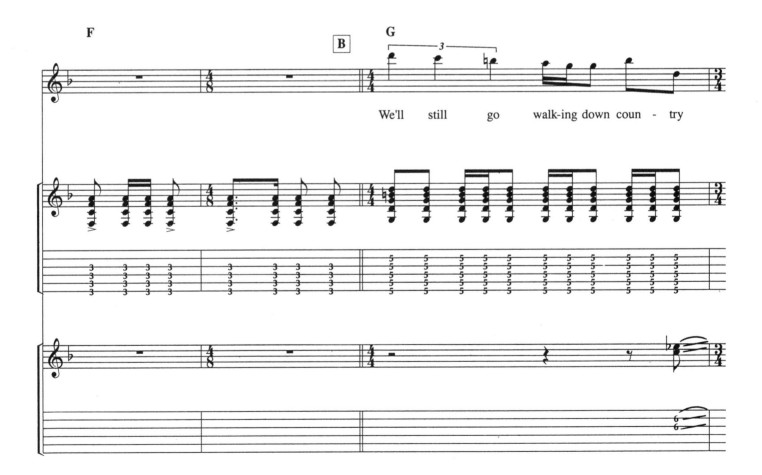

We'll still go walk-ing down coun - try

lanes, __ I'll sing the same old __ song, hear me call __ your name. __

FRIENDS

Words and Music by
JIMMY PAGE and ROBERT PLANT

World-Beat Symphonic Folk-Rock ♩ = 160 "double" Swing

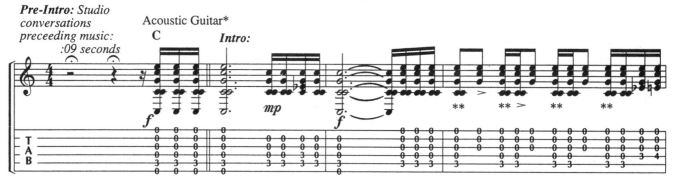

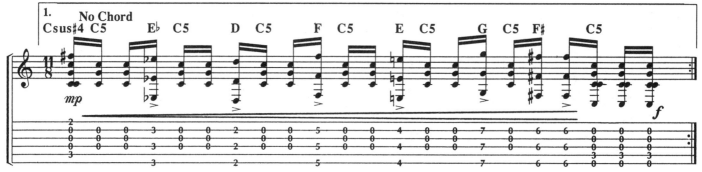

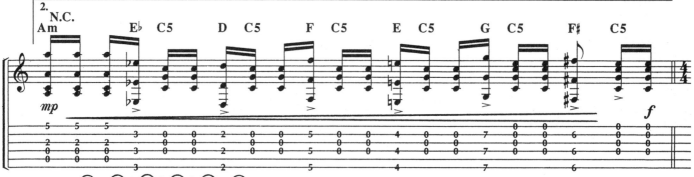

*C tuning: ⑥C, ⑤A, ④C, ③G, ②C, ①E.

**Let ring

***Chords alternate between C5, C minor, and Csus9/#11.

Verse 1:

*Let ring. Double-time "swing" feel throughout section.
**Continue with varied accent intensity on all upbeats throughout Verse and Chorus.

52

Chorus:

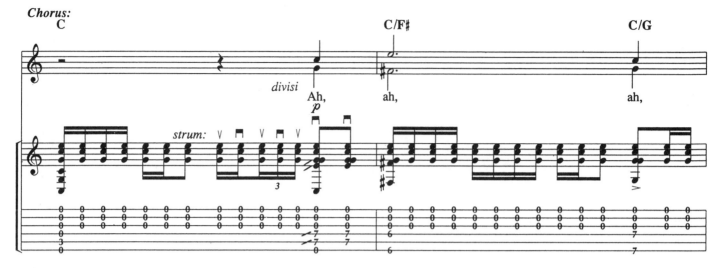

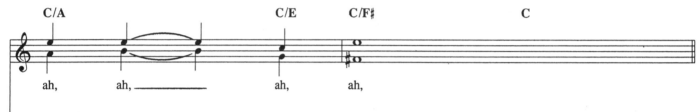

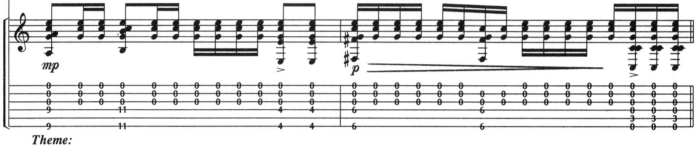

Theme:

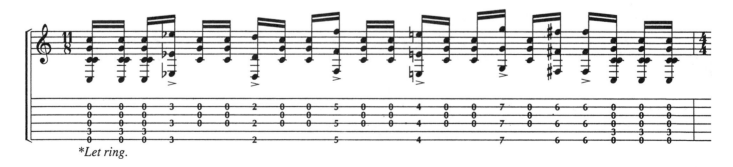

Let ring.

Mmm,___ I'm___ tel-lin' you___ now, the great-est thing you ev-er can do___ now

is trade a smile with some-one who's blue now,_____ it's ver-y eas-y just ah.

Verse 2:

Met a man___ on the road___ side cry - in', with-out a friend there's no___ de - ny - in',

Let ring

*Quickly hammer fingers on to ⑥ and ④ (muting ⑤) and begin slide up to VII.

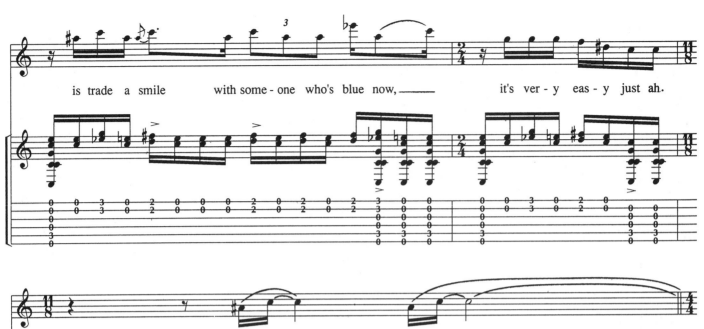

is trade a smile with some-one who's blue now,_____ it's ver-y eas-y just ah.

Oh,_____ yeah,_____

Coda:

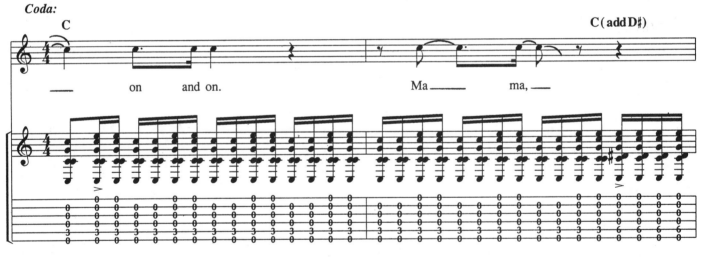

_____ on and on. Ma_____ ma,_____

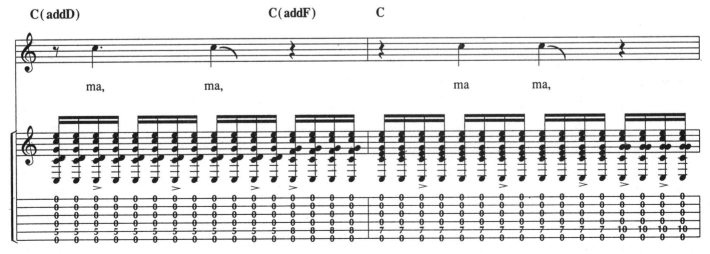

ma, ma, ma ma,

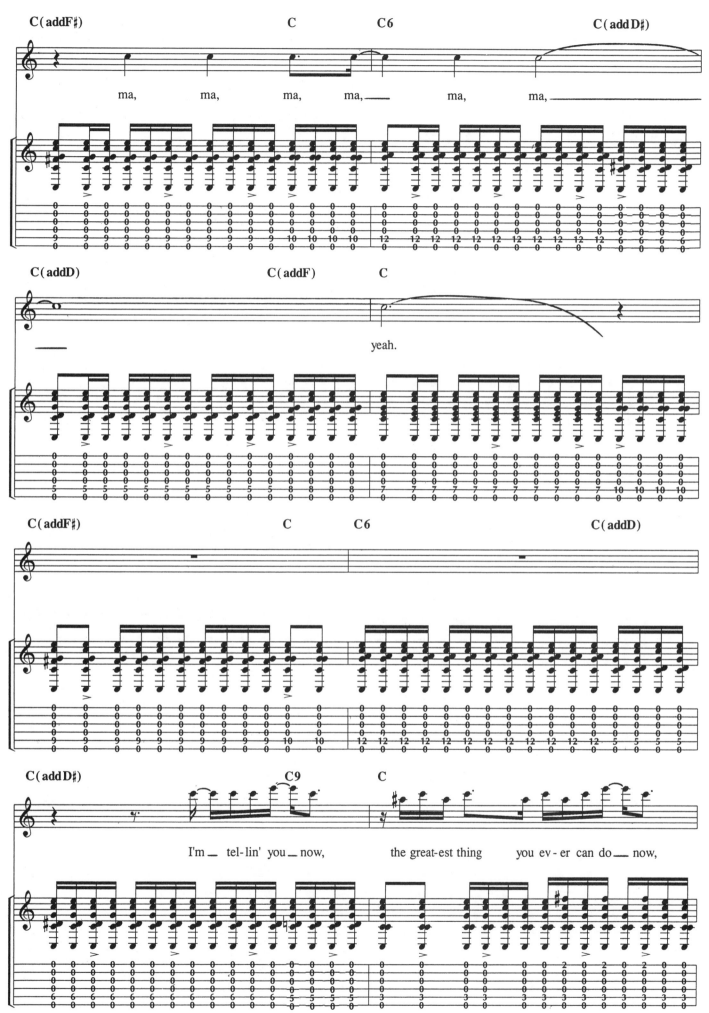

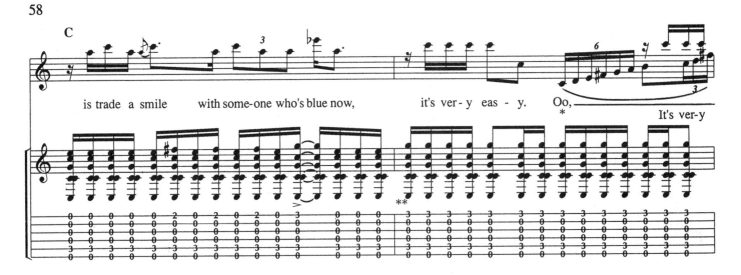

is trade a smile   with some-one who's blue now,   it's ver-y eas - y.   Oo, ————————   It's ver-y

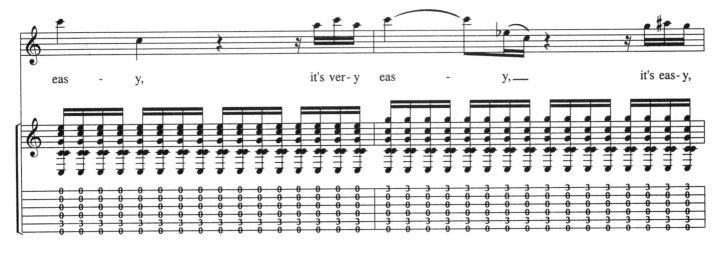

eas - y,   it's ver-y   eas   -   y, ——   it's eas-y,

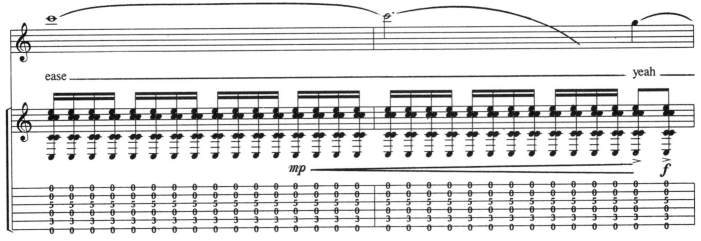

ease —— yeah ————

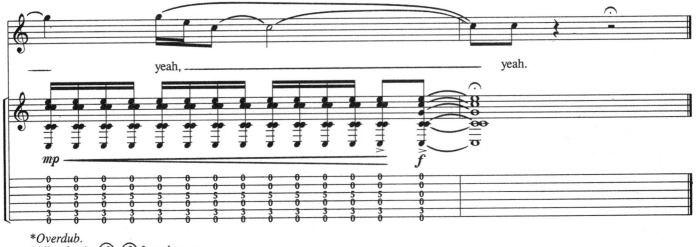

——   yeah, ————————————————————————————————————— yeah.

*Overdub.
**Emphasize ⑥-③ from here on.

STAIRWAY TO HEAVEN

Words and Music by
JIMMY PAGE and ROBERT PLANT

Capo at VII using a cutaway guitar with easy access to the 22nd fret. All notes in TAB at VII are open strings.

**The open first string is not played here, but rings sympathetically.*

***A gradual decrescendo continues for the next four measures to allow for the entrance of the recorders.*

Verse:

There's a la - dy who's sure, all that glit - ters is gold and she's

*The actual pitch of this note(e) is one octave higher

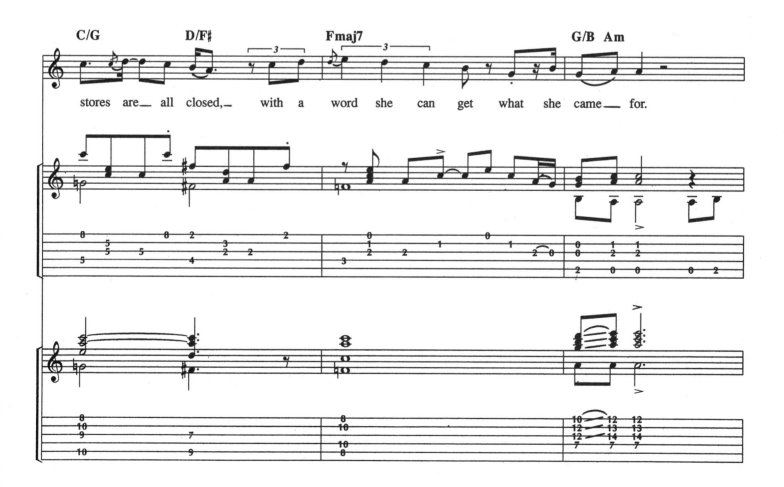

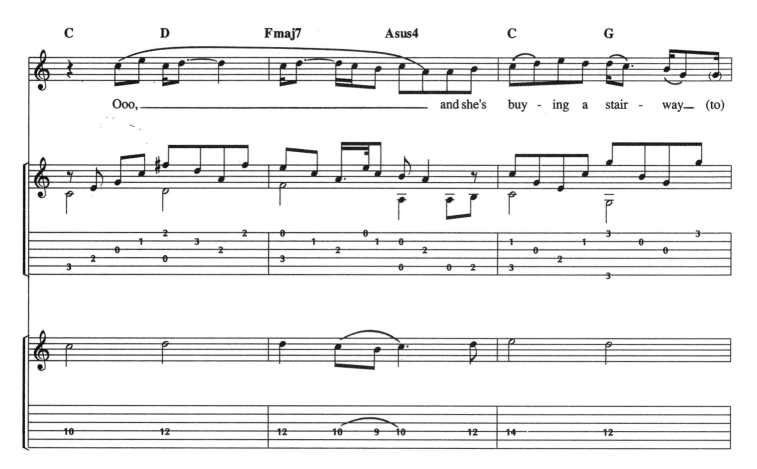

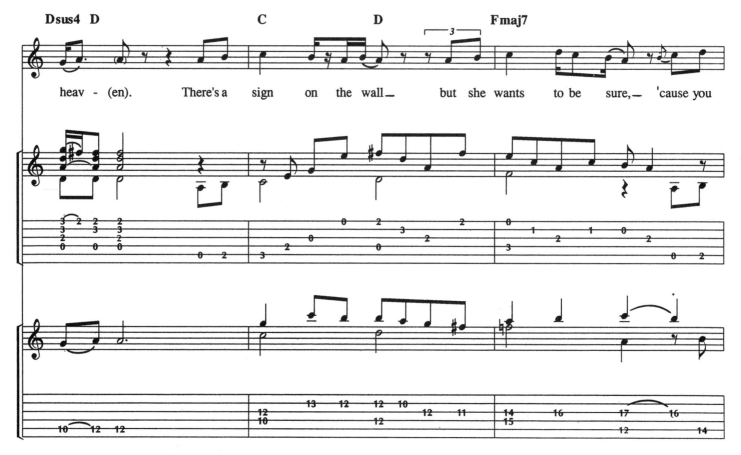

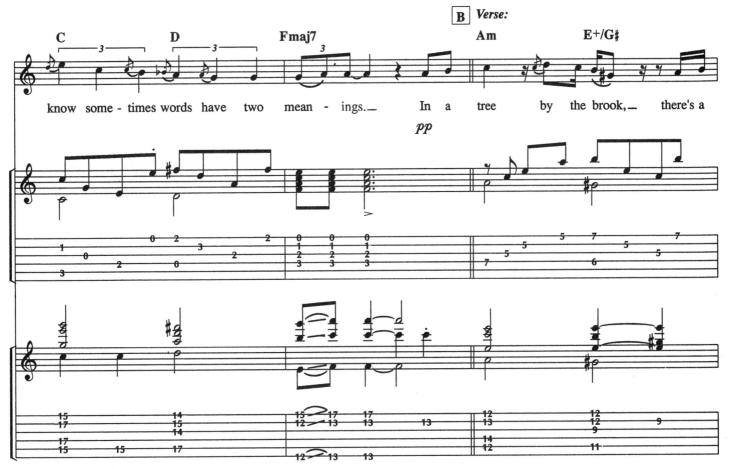

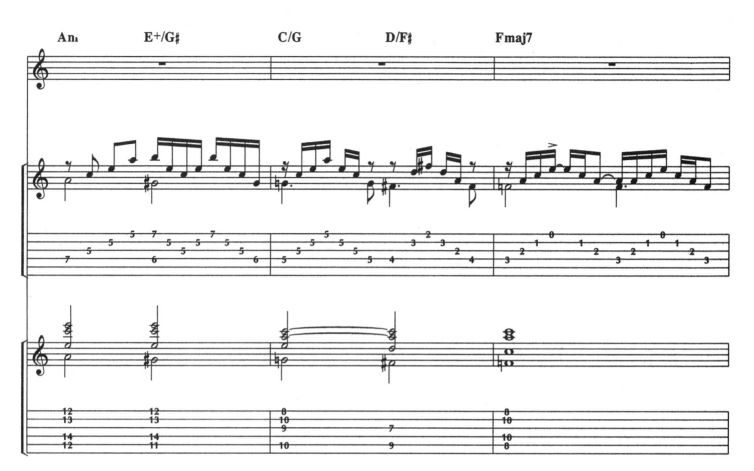

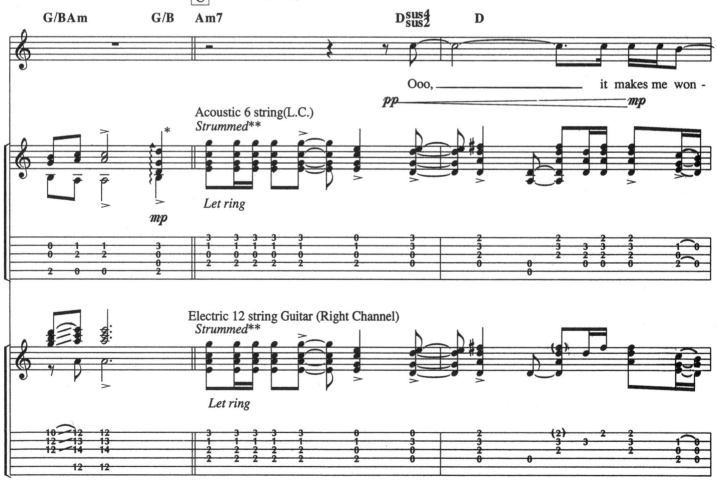

*The Acoustic Guitar is multi-tracked from here on.
**With a pick.

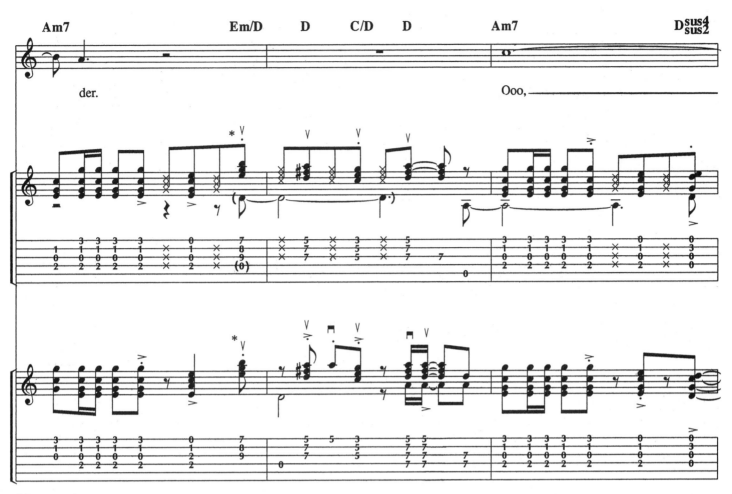

*Suggested strum

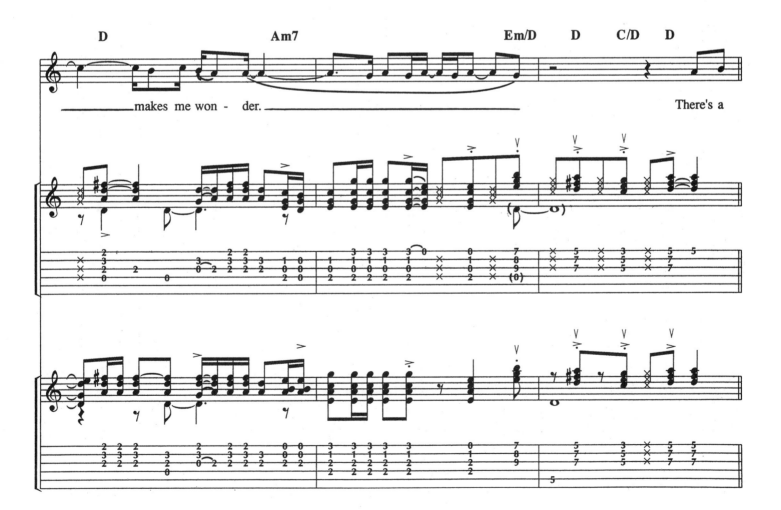

feel - ing I get___ when I look to the west,___ and my spir - it is cry - ing for leav-

Let ring

Rhythm Figure 1

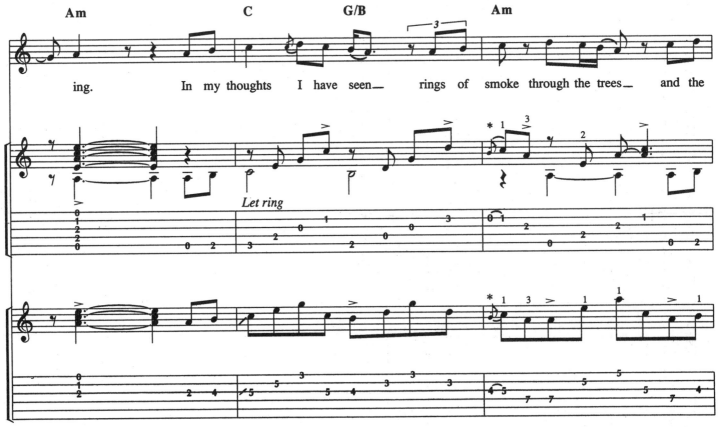

ing. In my thoughts I have seen___ rings of smoke through the trees___ and the

Let ring

Suggested fingering.

**T=Thumb on ⑥

* *Strings* ④ *and* ② *are muted while* ③ *and* ① *are open.*

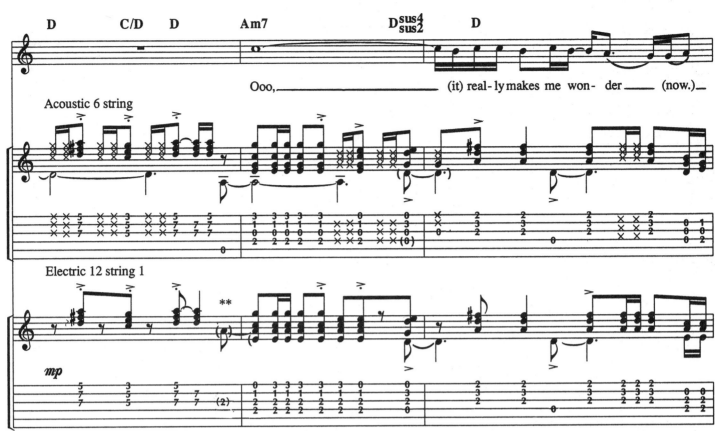

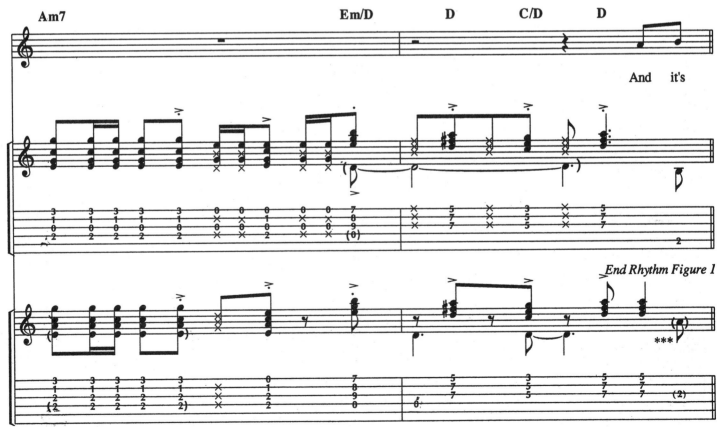

**Separate track – Sustain and fade over.

***Separate track.

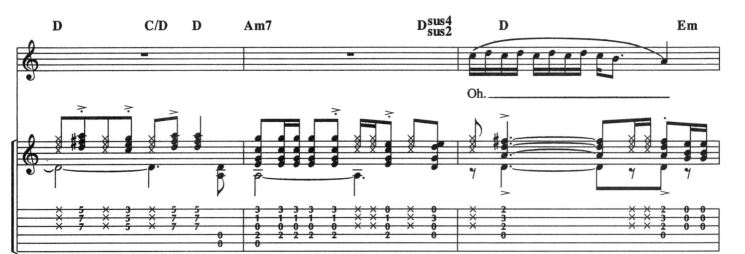

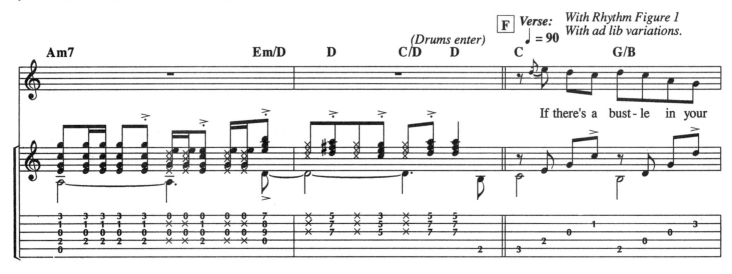

*Doubled with an Electric 6 string (Telecaster?) from here on.

And it makes me won - der.

Ahh. _____

G Verse: With Rhythm Figure 1
With ad lib variations.

Your head is hum - ming and it won't go, in case you don't know,

**( ) Acoustic Guitar track only.

C   G/B   Fmaj7   Am   C   G/B

the pip - er's call - ing you___ to join___ him.   Dear la - dy can you hear the wind-

Am   C   G/B   Fmaj7 Am

Rhythm figure 1 out

blow,   and did you__ know,___   your stair-way lies on the whis - 'prin' wind.___

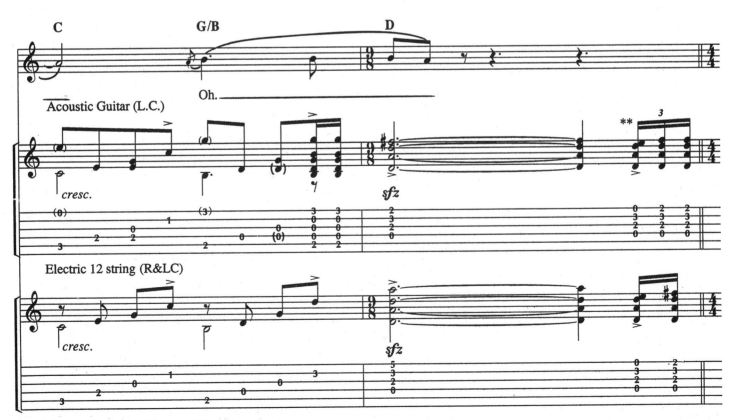

C   G/B   D

Oh._____

Acoustic Guitar (L.C.)

cresc.   *sfz*

Electric 12 string (R&LC)

cresc.   *sfz*

**The tempo is resumed by a cue from the guitarist.

*Notes in parenthesis are upper notes of quieter background track.

I *Bridge:(Guitar Solo)*

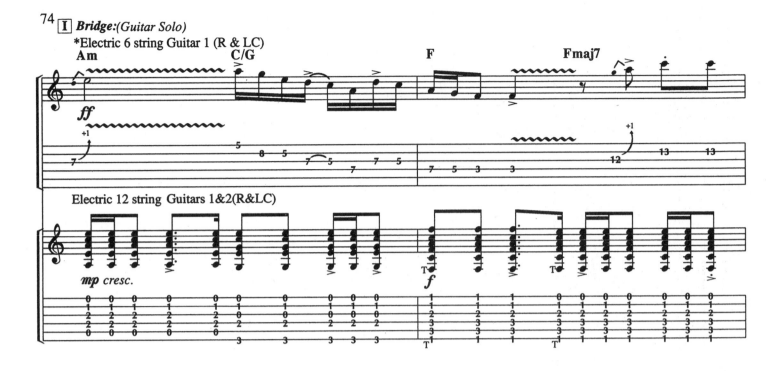

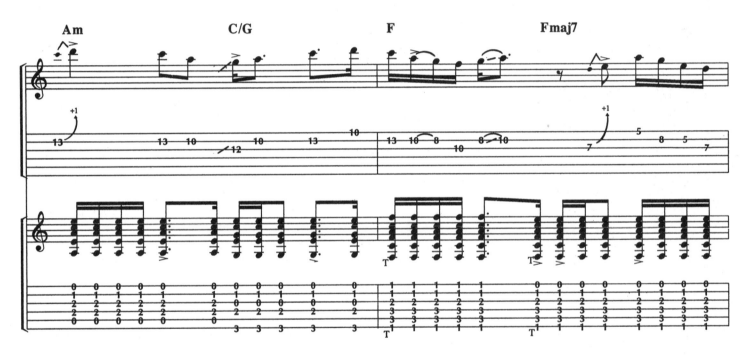

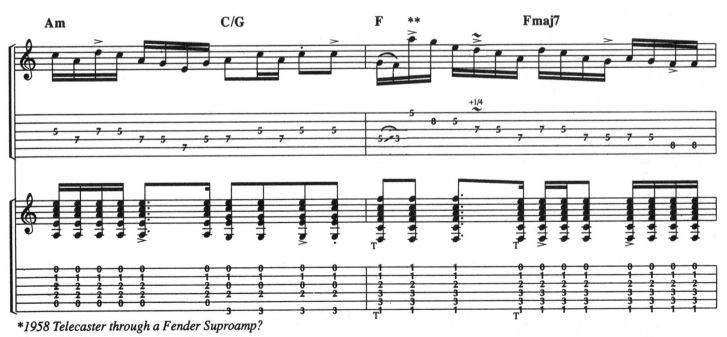

*1958 Telecaster through a Fender Suproamp?

** punch in from a separate track

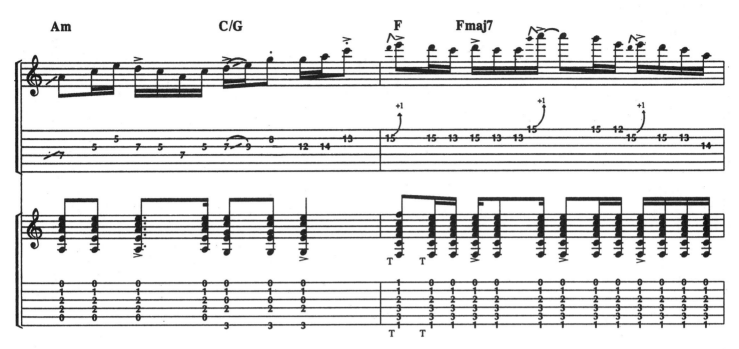

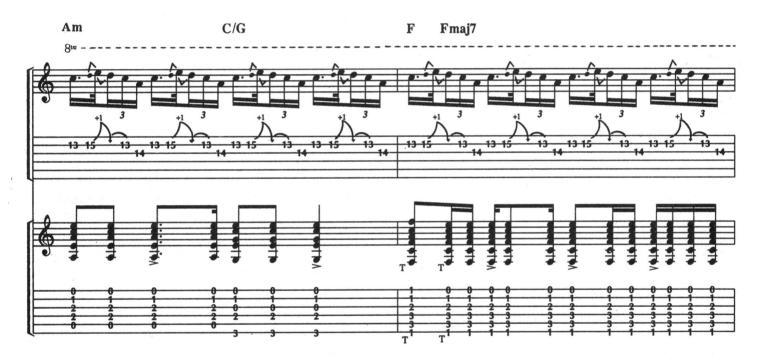

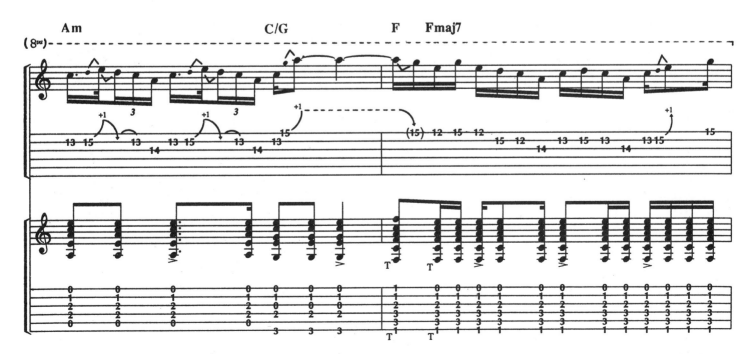

*Played with a glass or metal slide.

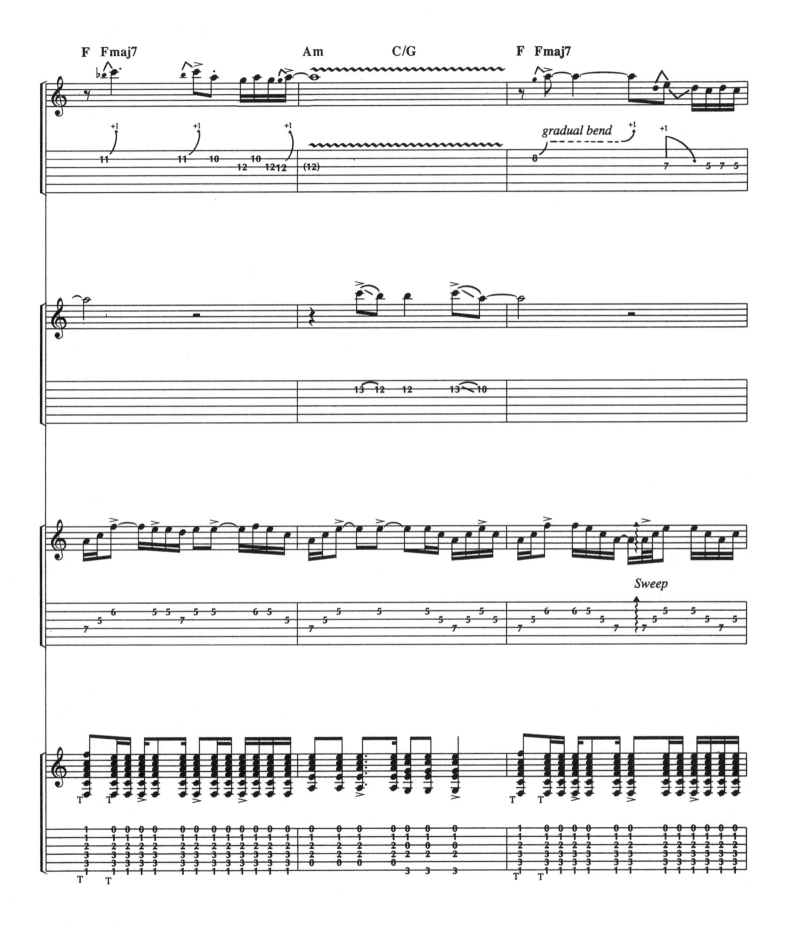

J **Verse:** *With Rhythm Figure 3 with ad lib variations*

♩ = 102

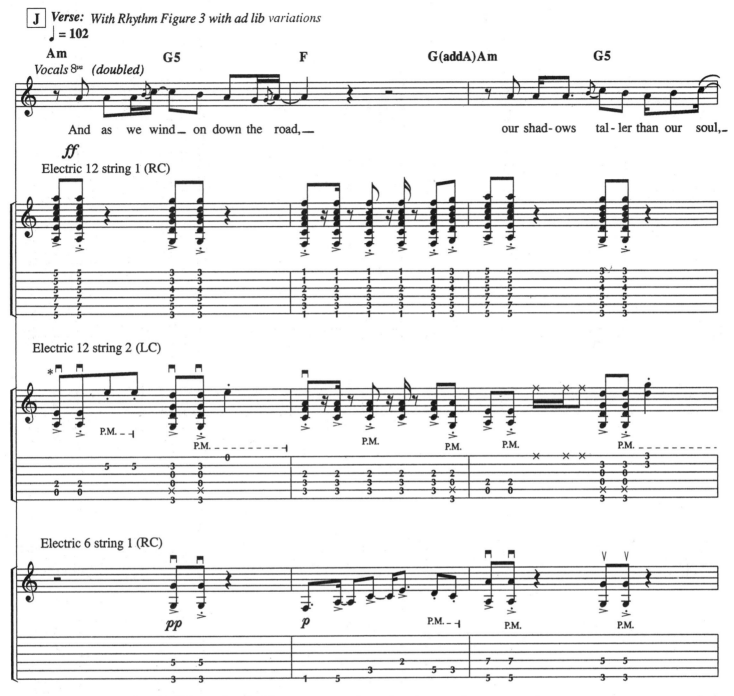

*Palm muting is alternated (off then on) as in this two measure phrase from here on, but not notated.

Rhythm Figure 3
Electric 12 string Guitar 3 (RC)

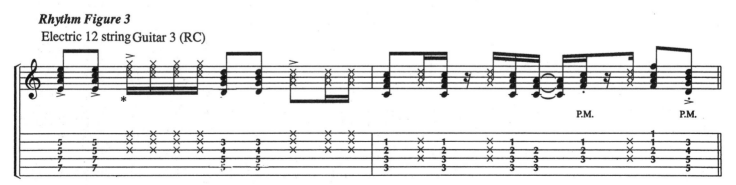

*Mute strings with fret hand at current chord position.

Right and left channels from here on.

gold._____ And if you lis - ten ver - y hard,_____

*Pan to center.
**Doubling ends.

Lead vocal in downstems, distorted chorus track in upstems.

*Pre-bent from here on

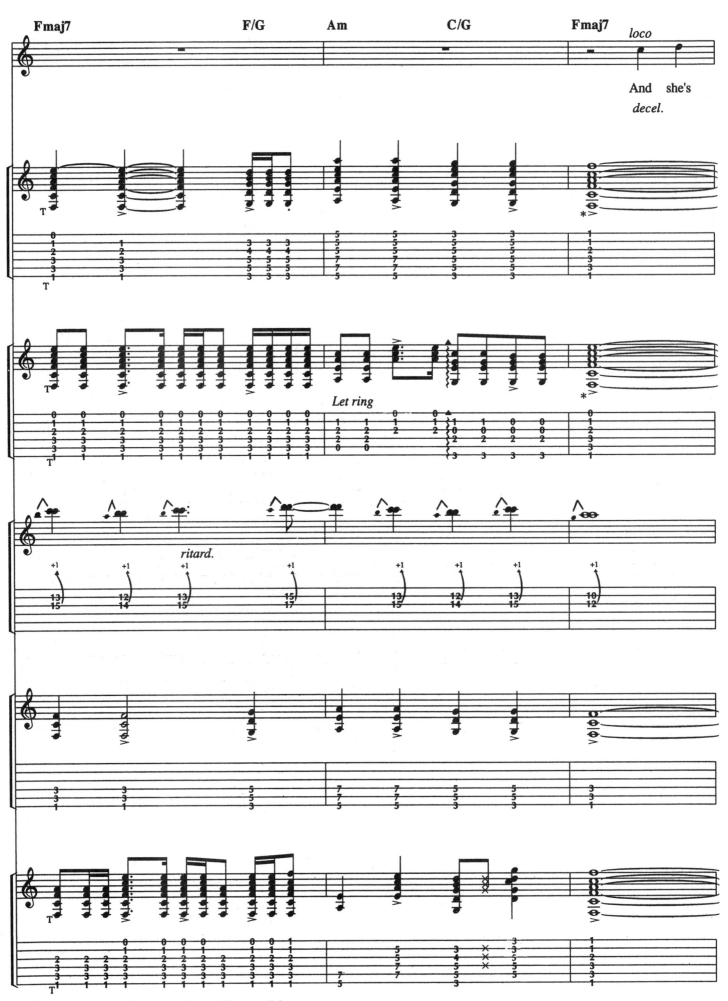

*VSO (variable speed/pitch oscilator) 1/2 step glide.

Fade out

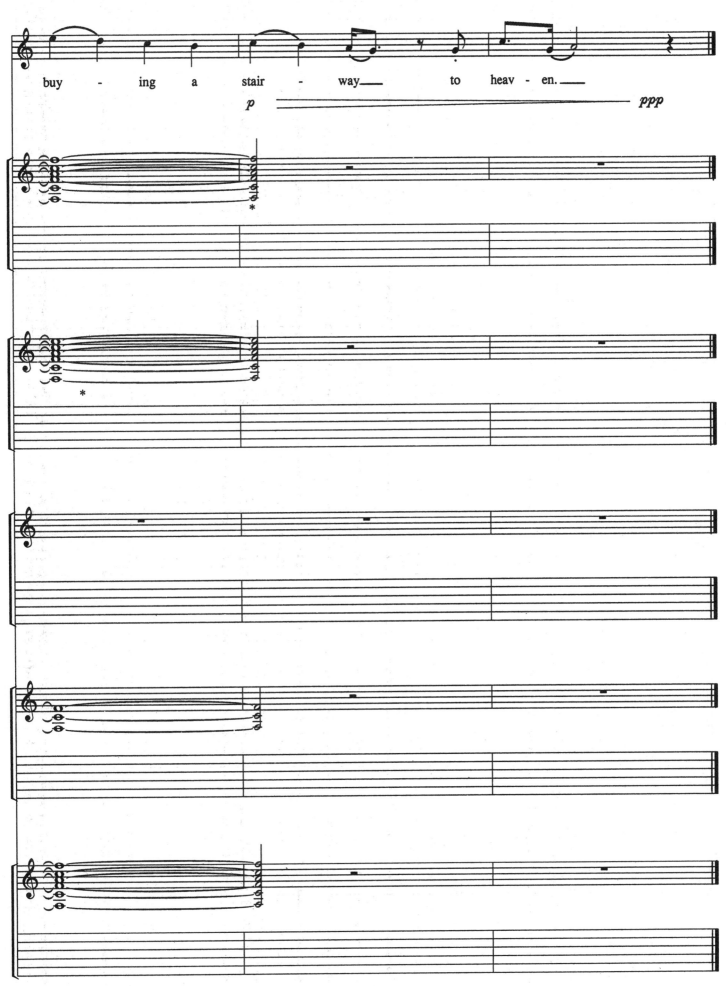

buy - ing a stair - way___ to heav - en. ___

p ———————————— *ppp*

Oscillate guitar volume knob rhythmically.

GOING TO CALIFORNIA

Words and Music by
JIMMY PAGE and ROBERT PLANT

Tuning: ⑥ = D, ⑤ = A, ④ = D, ③ = G, ② = B, ① = D.

**Both Mandolins are arranged for Guitars in the above tuning that are capoed at VII.
All notes at VII are notated as open in the TAB.

Spent my days___ with a wom-an un-kind,___ smoked my stuff___ and

Suggested fingering: ⑥ = *second finger,* ① = *third finger.*

End Mandolin 1 Figure 1

End Mandolin 2 Figure 1

B *Verse:*
With Mandolins 1 & 2 Figures 1

Made up my mind, — make a new start, — goin' Cal - i - for - nia with an

ach - in', — in my heart. —

Notes in parenthesis may be an overdubbed jaw harp, or EQ effect.

Dsus4   **D**

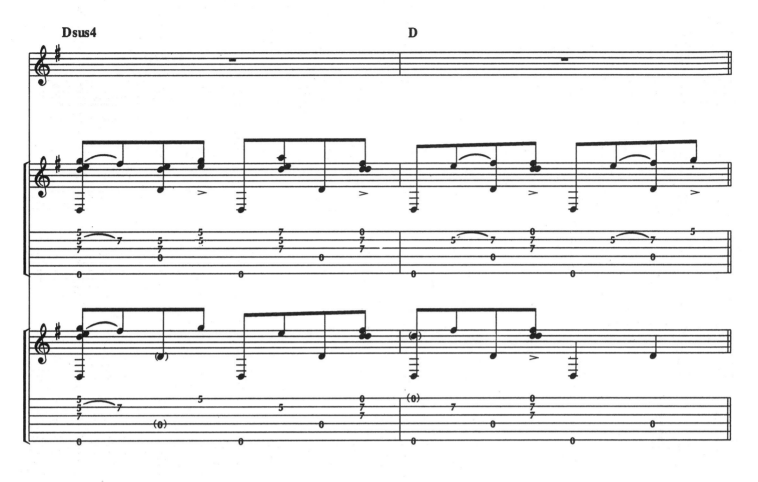

C *Verse:*

With Mandolins 1 & 2 Figures 1

G   **Gmaj7**   **G6**   **G**   **Gmaj7**

Some-one told__ me there's a girl out there,__ with love in her eyes,__ and

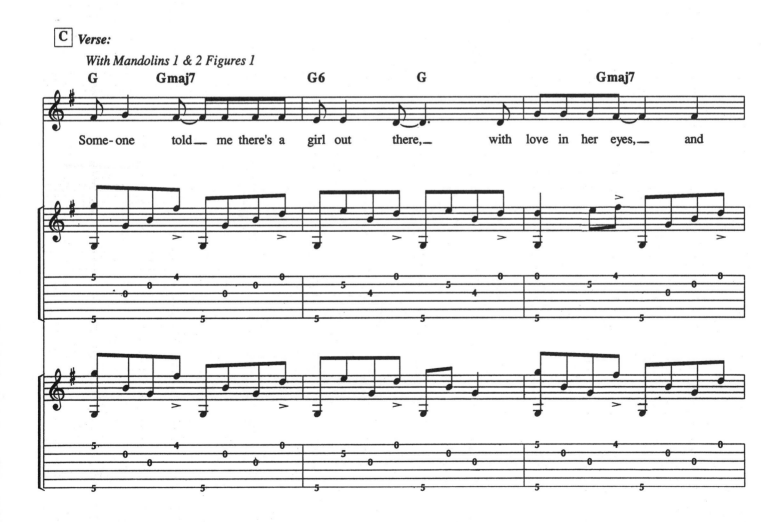

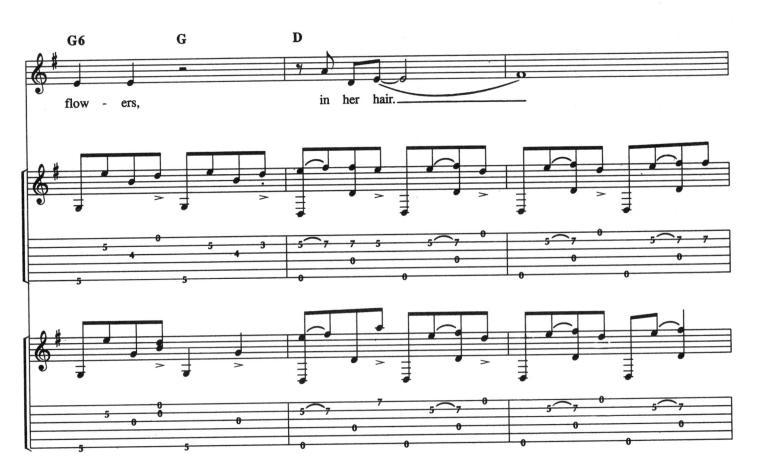

flow - ers, in her hair.

End Guitar 1 Figure 1

E Verse:
With Mandolin 2 Figure 1 & Guitar 1 Figure 1

Took my chances on a big jet plane, nev - er let them tell ya' that they're

Mandolin 1

Guitar 2

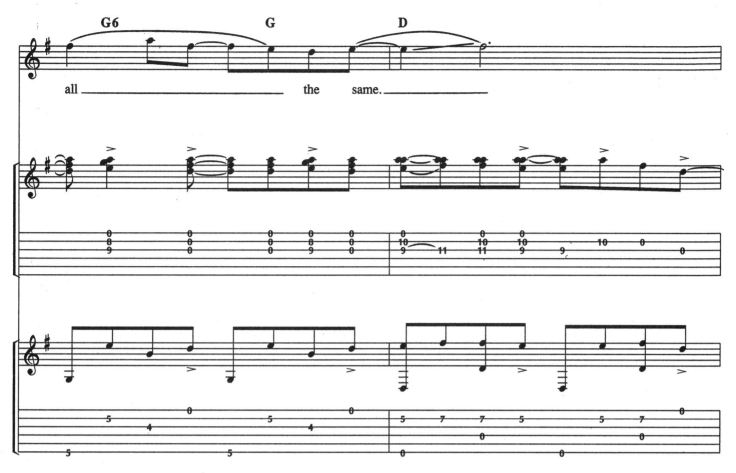

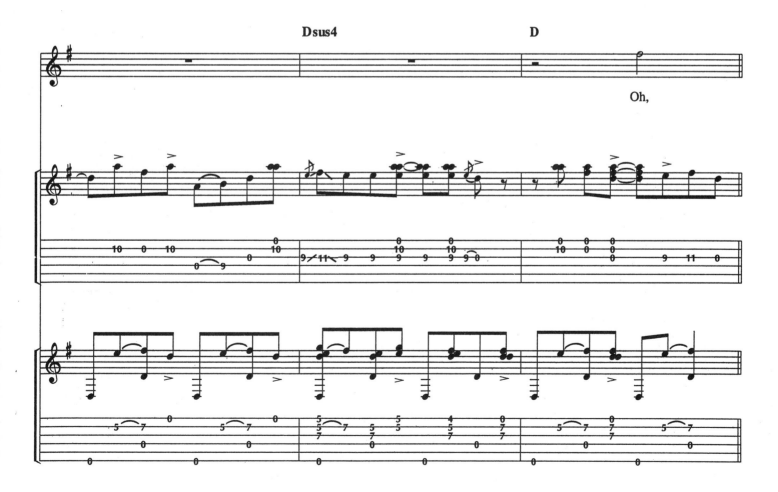

G *Verse:*
With Mandolin 2 Figure 1 & Guitar 1 Figure 1

Moun-tains and the can-yons start to trem-ble and shake,___ child-ren of the sun be-gin___

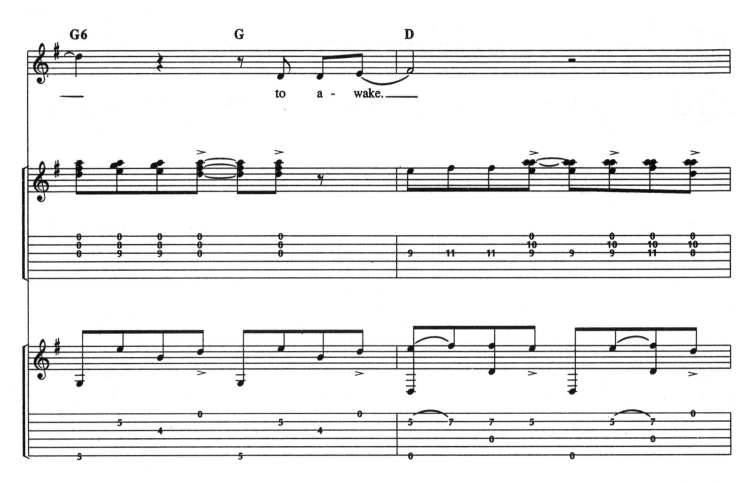

to a - wake._____

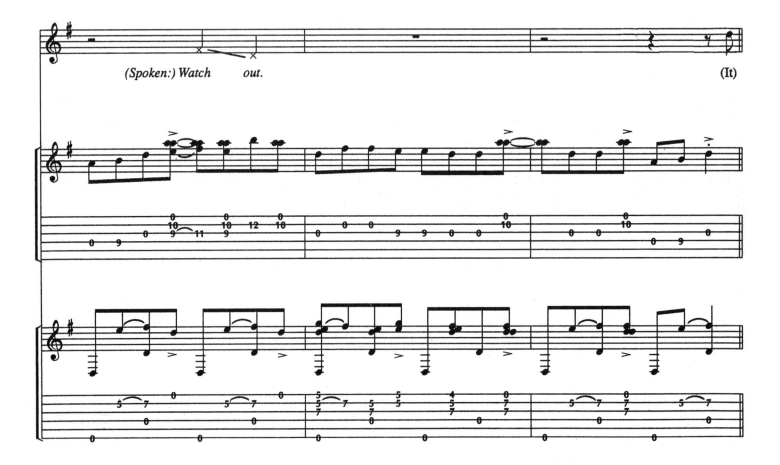

(Spoken:) Watch out.   (It)

seems that the wrath__ of the gods__ got a punch__ on the nose,__ and it start - ed to flow.__

__ I think I might be sink - in'.

*Strummed with the thumb instead of finger picked.
Notes in parentheses appear on one track only and may be omitted when impractical.

D

sings.____ La, la, la, la.

Dsus2   **D**   **D(addG)**   **D**   *End Guitar 2 Figure 2*

*

**

(0)

K *Verse:*
With Mandolin 1 & 2 Figures 1 and Guitar 2 Figure 2 (2 times) w/ ad lib variations

G   **Gmaj7**   **G6**   **G**   **Gmaj7**

Ride a white mare in the foot-steps of dawn. Tryin' to find a wo-man who's nev-

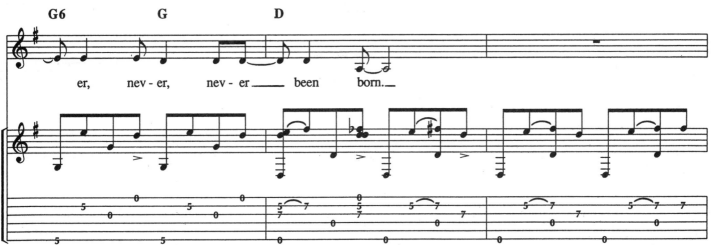

G6   **G**   **D**

er, nev-er, nev-er____ been born.____

*Upstrum with thumbnail.
**Upstrum with pad of finger.

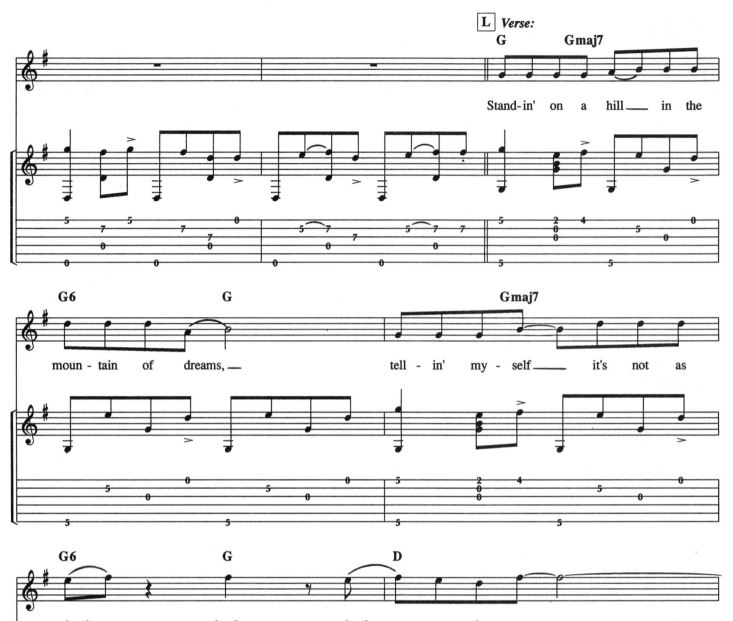

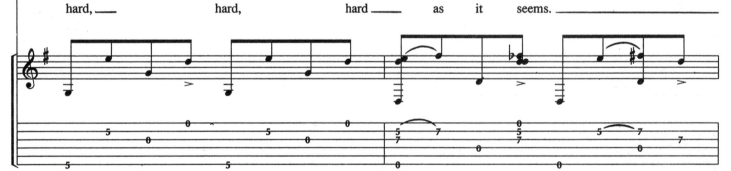

N *Outro:*
With Guitar 1 Figure 3 (to fade)

Guitar 3

Jaw Harp through reverse echo return.

Figure 3
Guitar 1

110

OVER THE HILLS AND FAR AWAY

Words and Music by
JIMMY PAGE and ROBERT PLANT

Moderately fast Rock (♩ = 98)
Intro:
Guitar 1* (Acoustic 6 string)

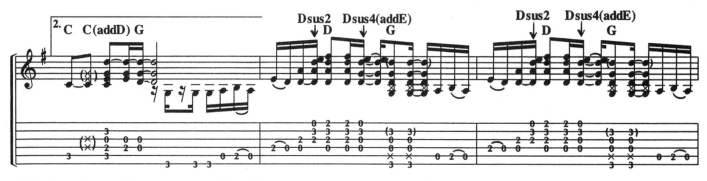

* 12 string guitar doubles on repeat and Verse 1.

Fill 1
Guitar 2 (12 string)

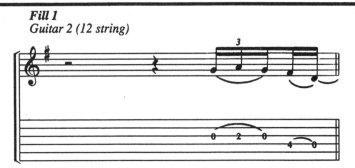

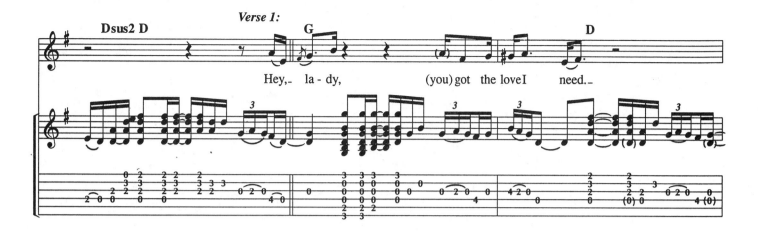

Verse 1:

Hey,— la - dy, (you) got the love I need.—

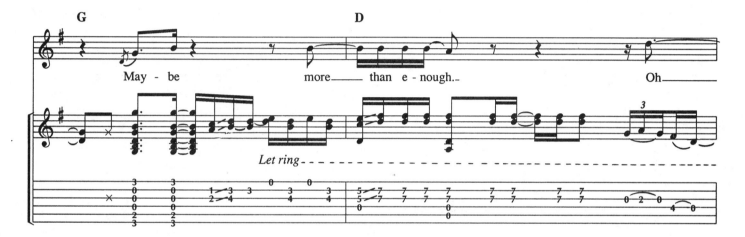

May - be more—— than e - nough.— Oh——

— dar-lin', dar - lin', dar-lin', walk a - while— with me.—

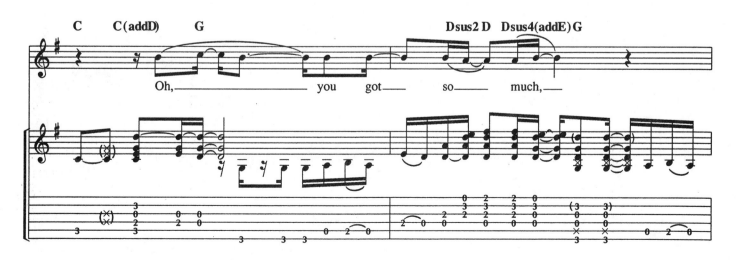

Oh,——————— you got— so— much,—

114

so   much,___

so___   much.___

Let ring-----

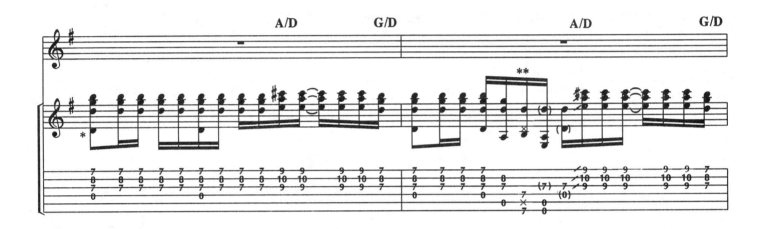

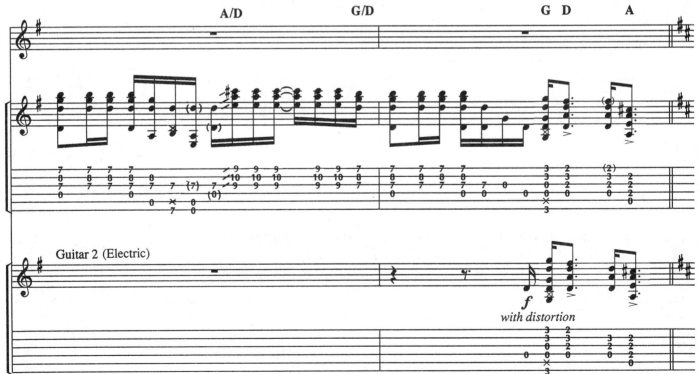

Enter Bass and Drums

Guitar 2 (Electric)

f
with distortion

Let 4th string ring out.
** With thumb.

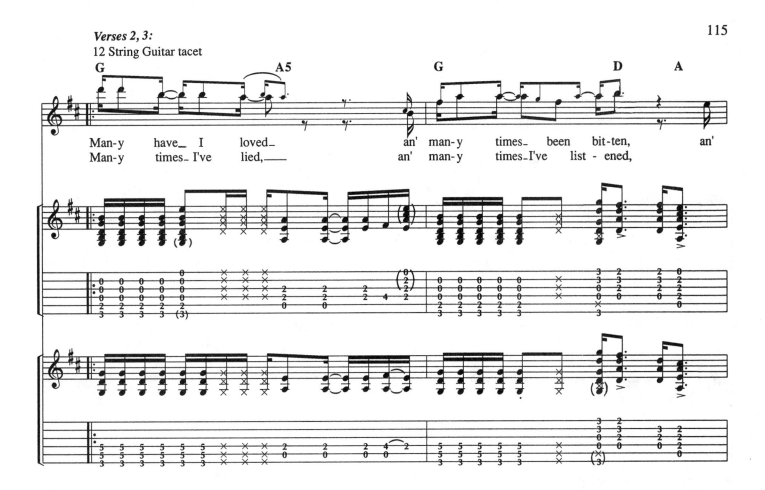

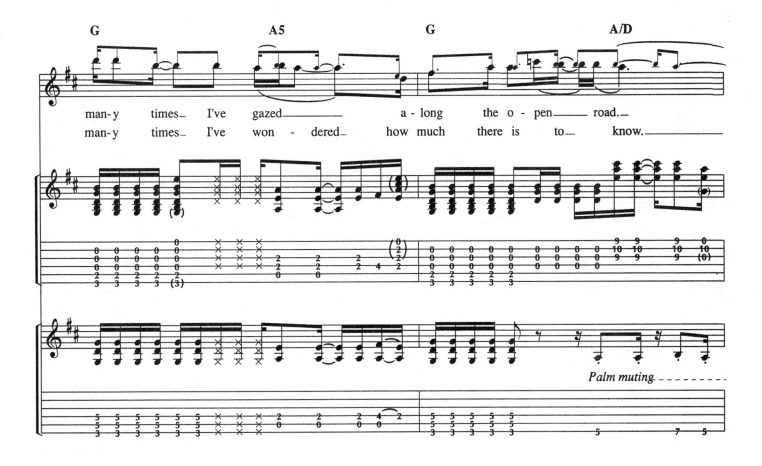

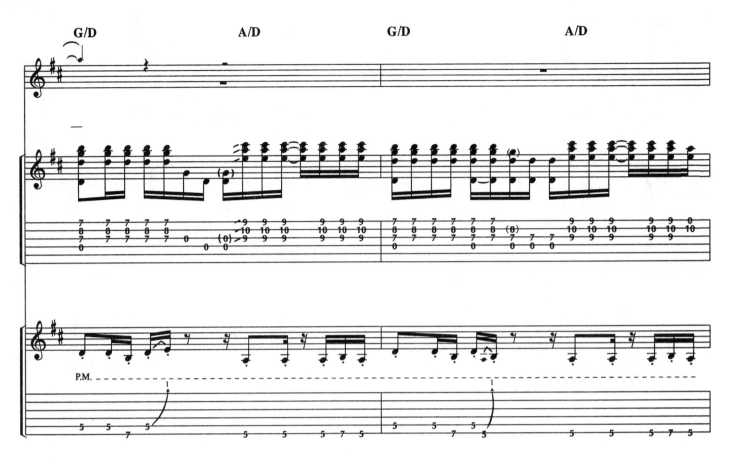

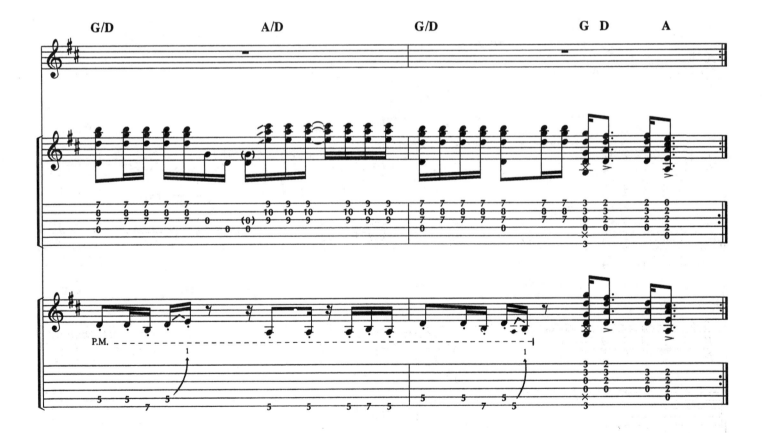

Verse 4:

Man-y dreams— come true, an' some have sil - ver lin - ings. I—

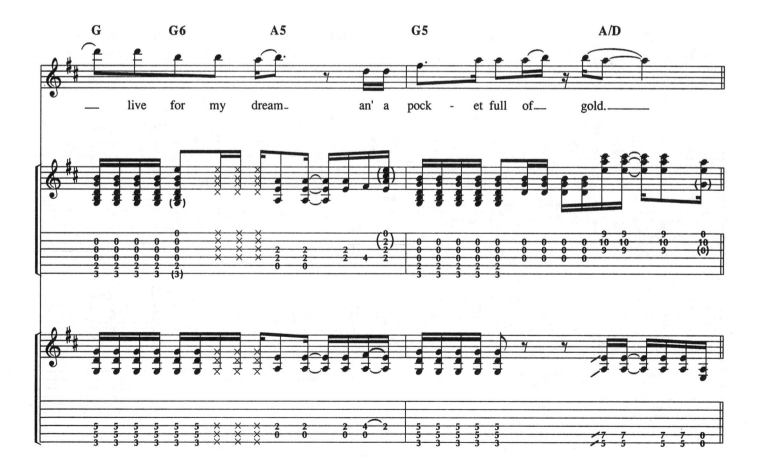

— live for my dream— an' a pock - et full of— gold.———

* Guitar 3-downstem notes
Guitar 4-upstem notes

(F♯)

Guitar 1

Guitar 2

Guitar 3

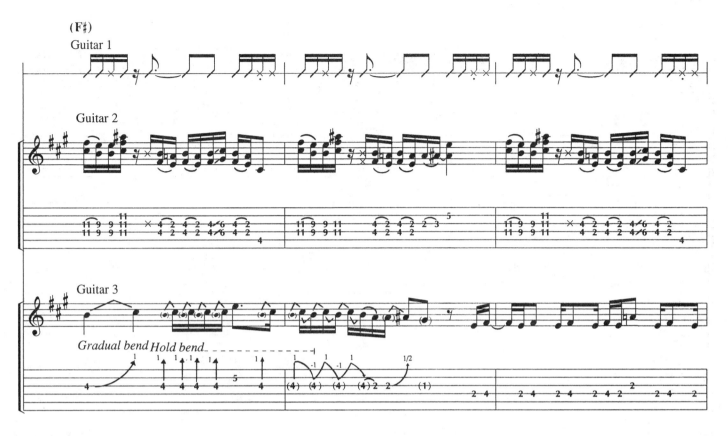

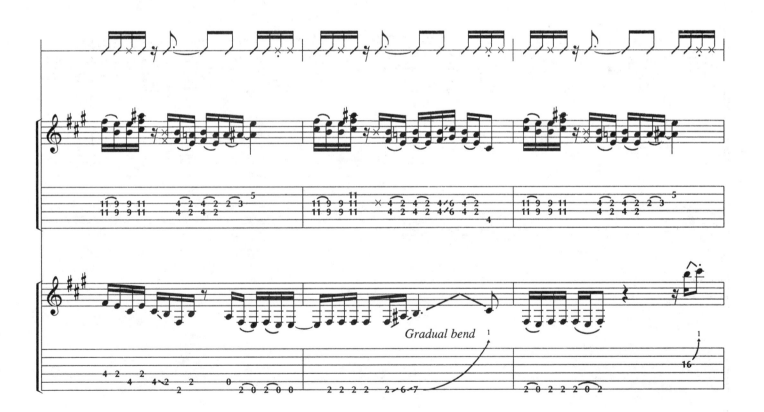

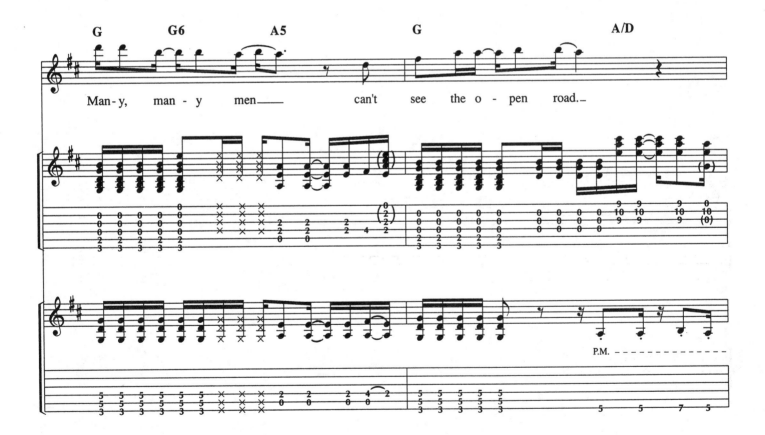

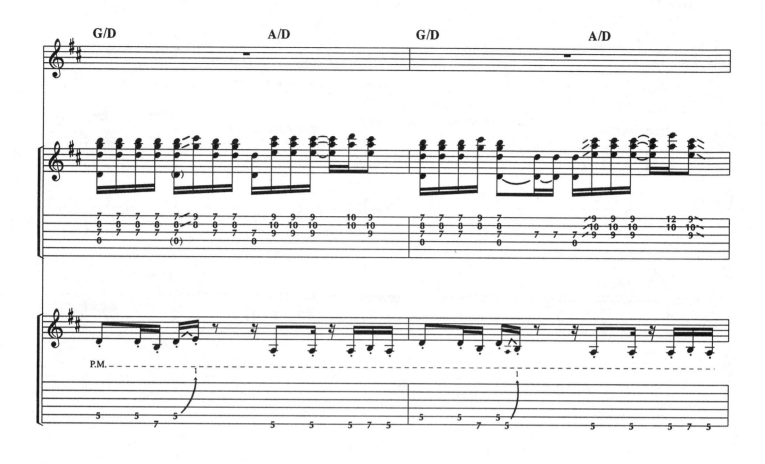

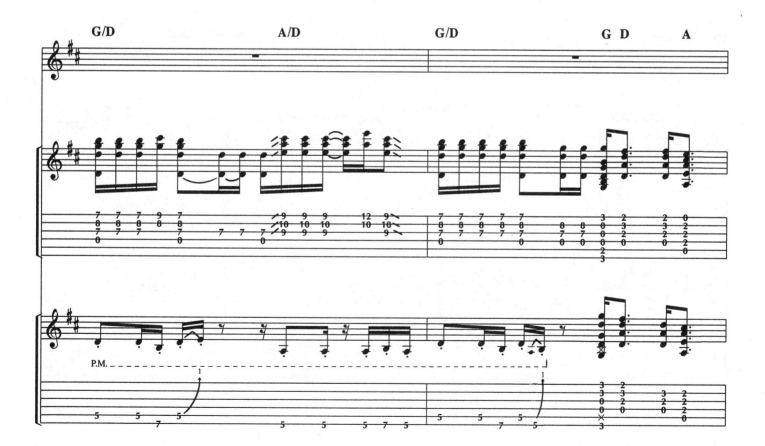

Verse 6:

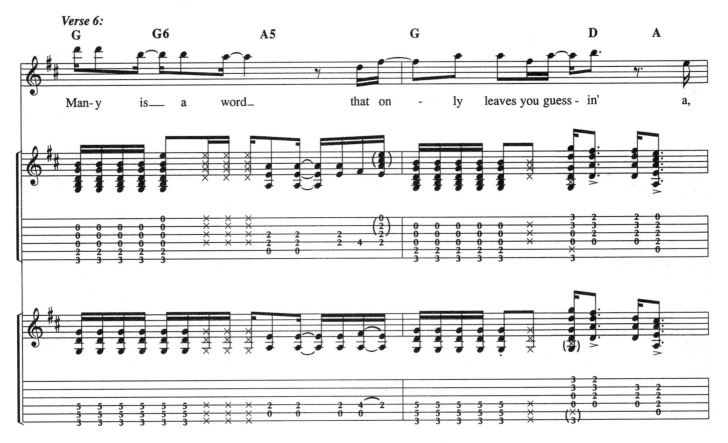

Man-y is__ a word__ that on - ly leaves you guess - in' a,

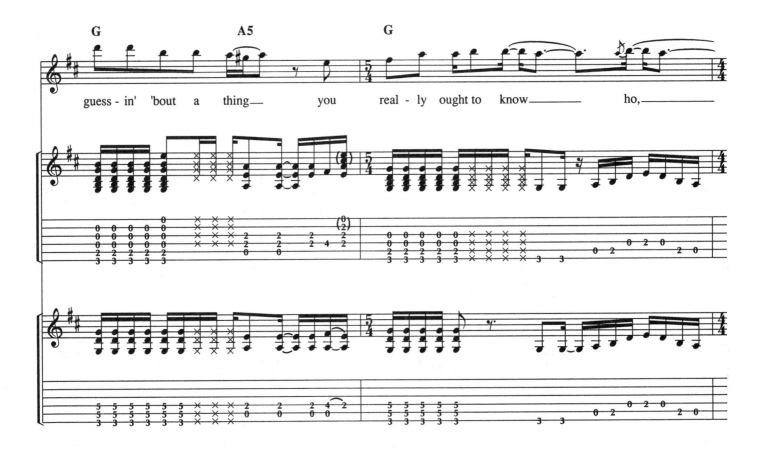

guess - in' 'bout a thing__ you real - ly ought to know__ ho,__

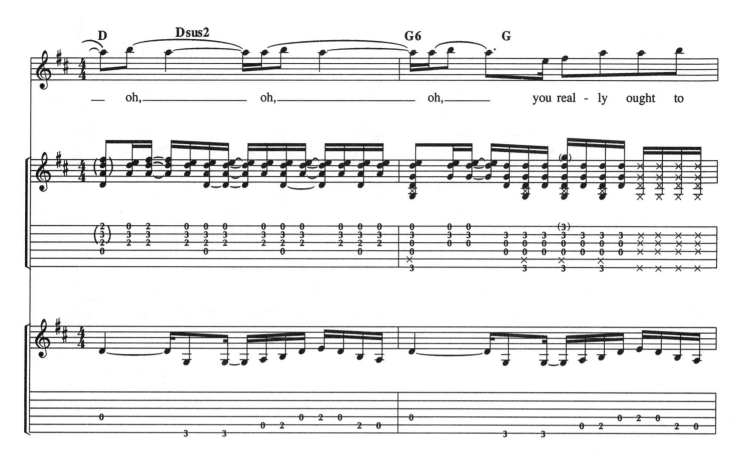

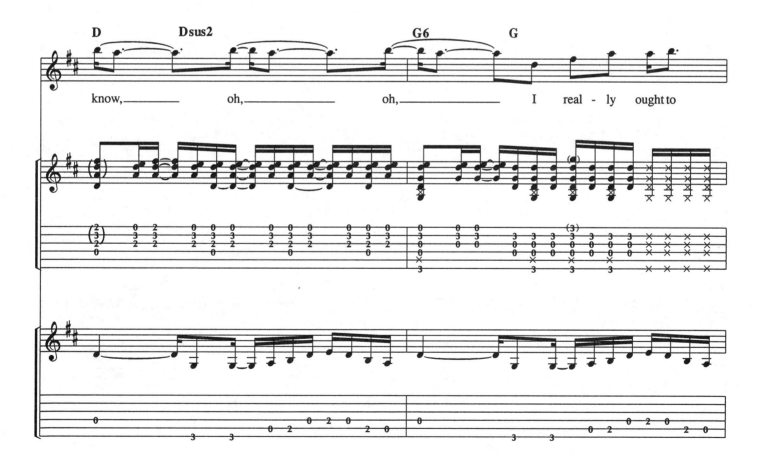

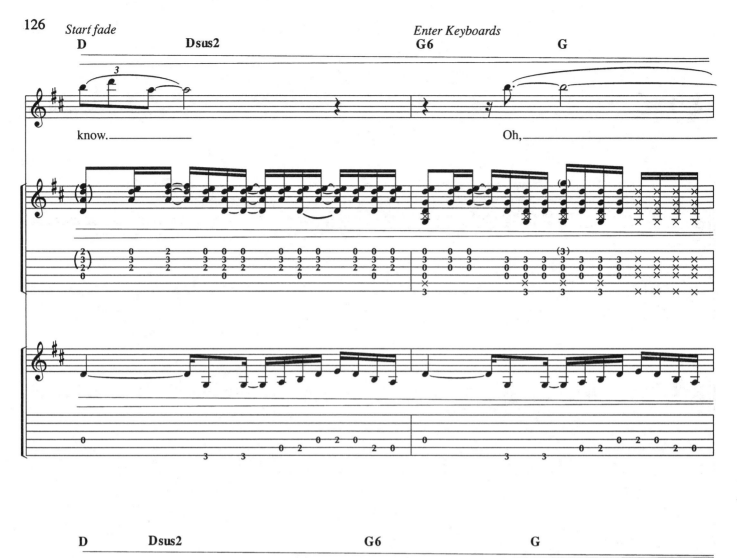

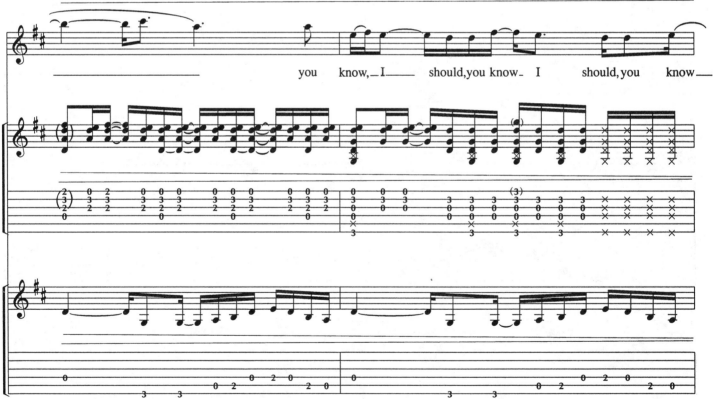

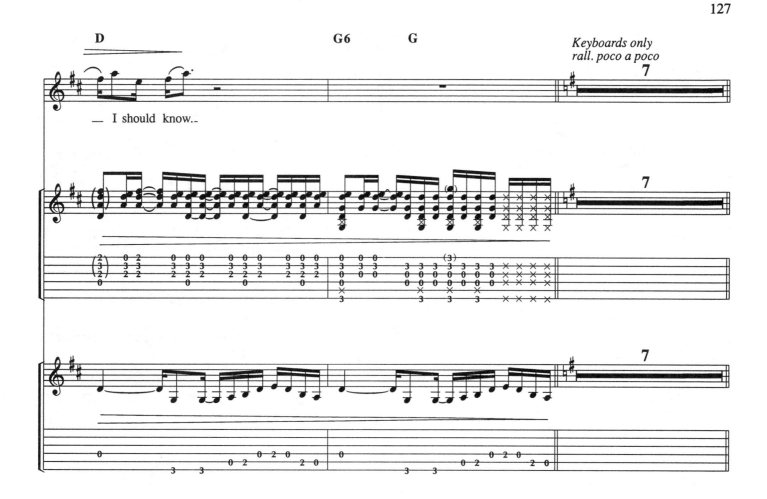

I should know..

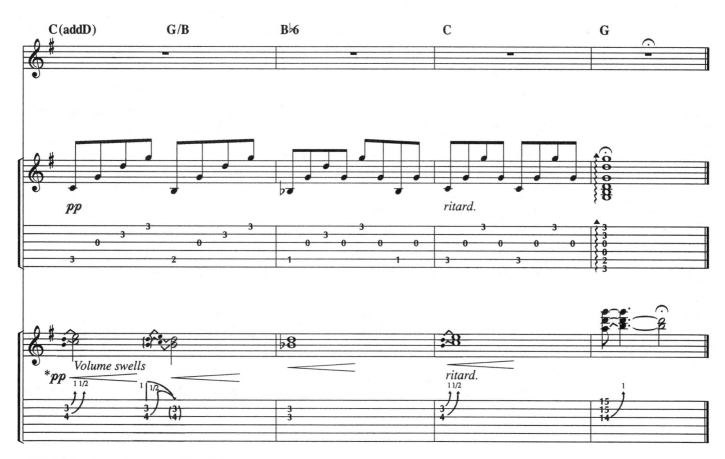

*Pedal Steel sounds arranged for Guitar.

TANGERINE

Words and Music by
JIMMY PAGE

Country Rock Ballad ♩ = 76
Warm-up:

Mandolin *(Arranged for Guitar) Capo at 5*

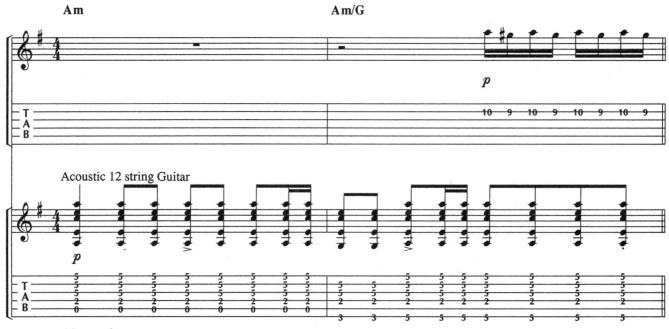

See performance notes

Spoken counting

"One   two   one two   three   four   one   two"
(Whispered)

Intro:
Acoustic 12 string Guitar

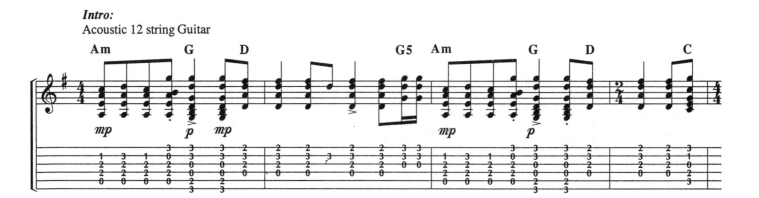

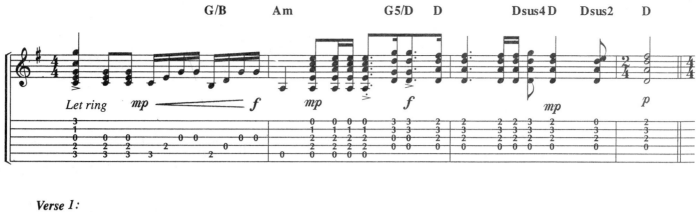

Verse 1:

Meas - ur - ing a sum - mers day, I on - ly find it slips a -

Mandolin *(Arranged for Guitar)*

Acoustic 12 string Guitar

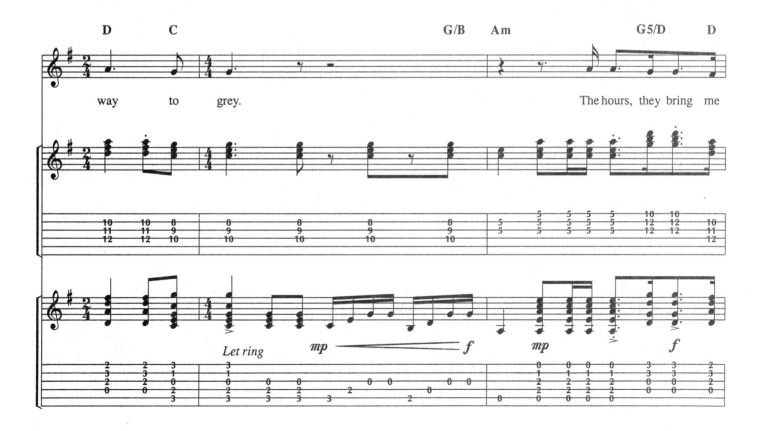

way to grey. The hours, they bring me

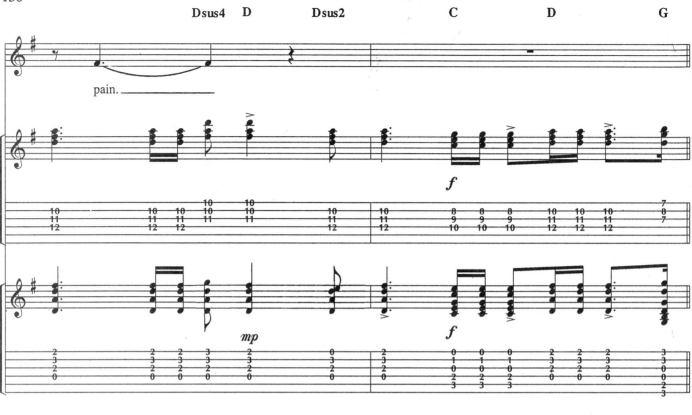

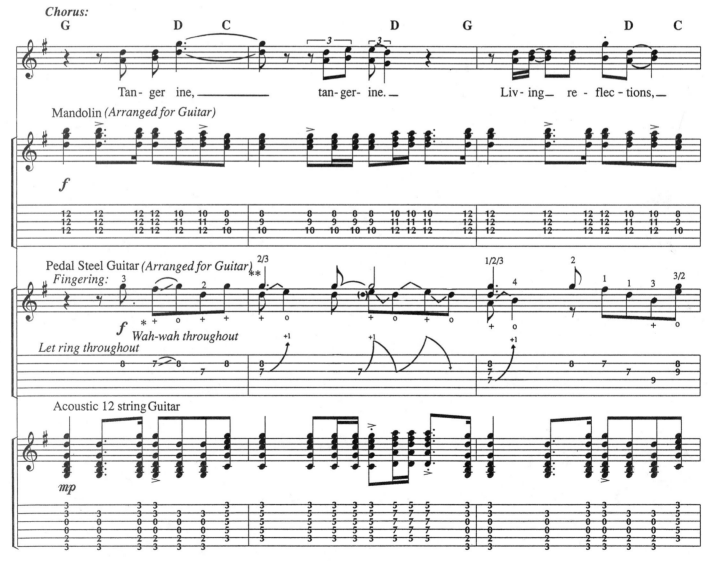

(+ = treble position, o = bass position)
** *The first number if for the finger on the lower string.*

* High G heard with chord is an overtone.

Verse 2:

Think-ing how it used to be. Does she still re-mem - ber times like

these? To think of us a-gain, and I do.

Bridge 1:
Mandolin

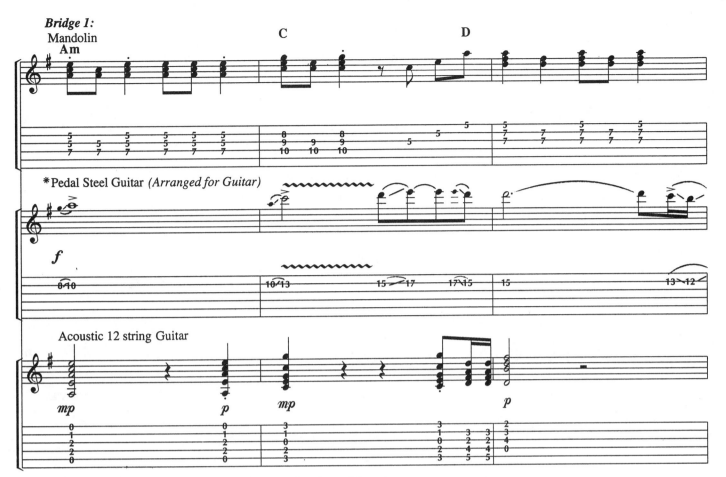

Pedal Steel Guitar (Arranged for Guitar)

Acoustic 12 string Guitar

* Using a metal slide will create a similar sound to the pedal steel.
Tuning: E A D G# B D

Chorus:

Tan - ger- ine, _____ Tan - ger- ine, _____ liv - ing __ re - flec - tions, _____

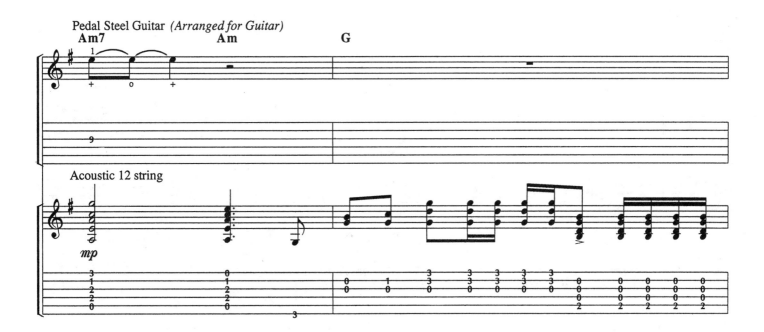

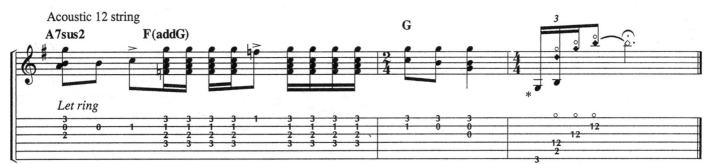

Hammer-on with 2nd then 1st left hand fingers for the bass notes G & B, with right hand classical style harmonics at XII.

THANK YOU

Words and Music by
JIMMY PAGE and ROBERT PLANT

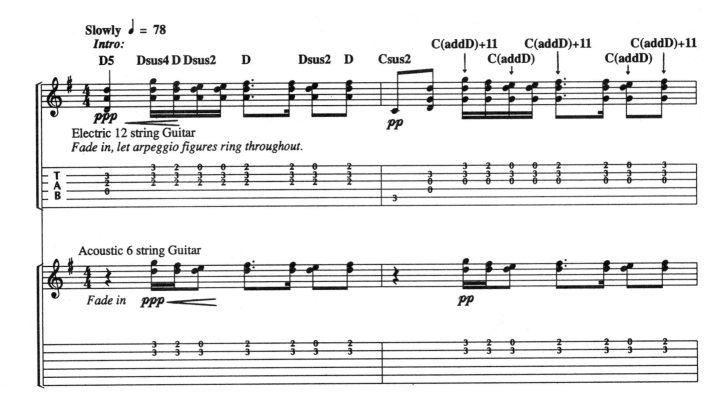

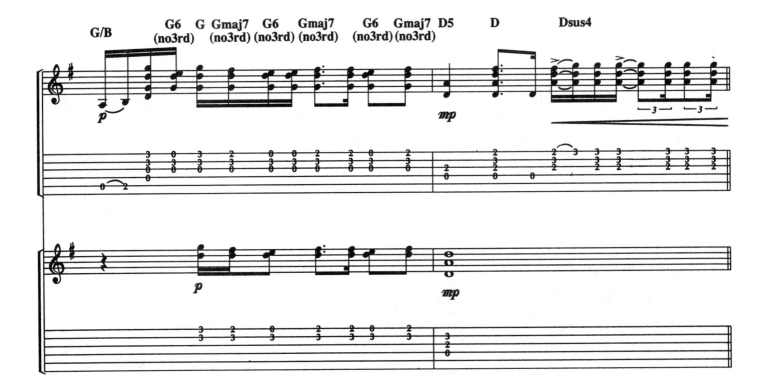

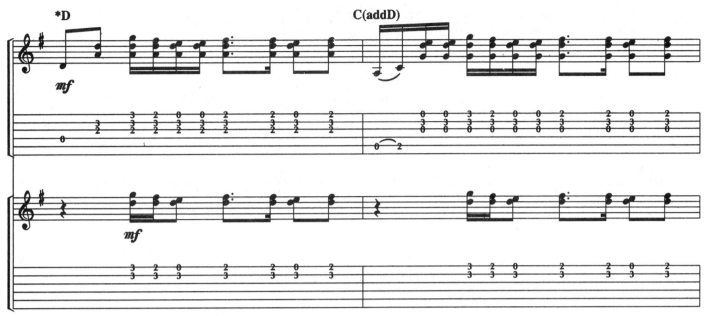

Chord symbols reflect primary harmonic movements.

Verse 1:

If the sun re - fused to shine, I would still be lov - in' you.

Parenthesized chords implied by Organ.

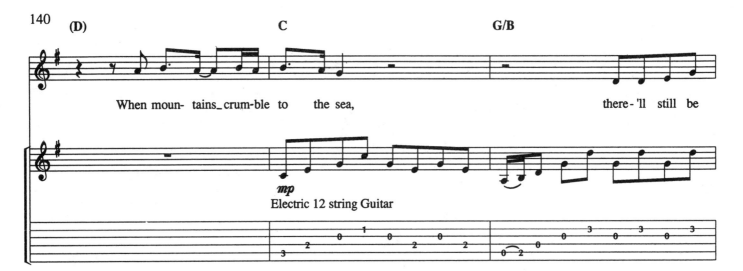

When moun- tains crum-ble to the sea, there-'ll still be

Electric 12 string Guitar

you and me. Kind wom-an I give you

my all. Kind wom-an noth-ing more.

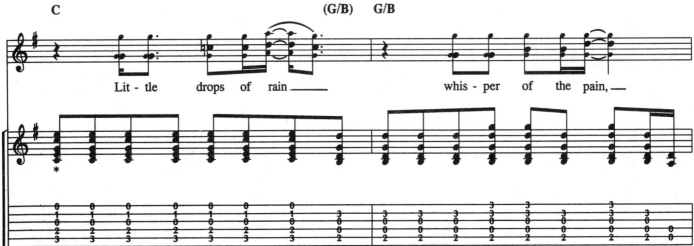

Lit - tle drops of rain whis - per of the pain,

*Doubled by acoustic 6-string Guitar

*Doubled by acoustic 6-string Guitar

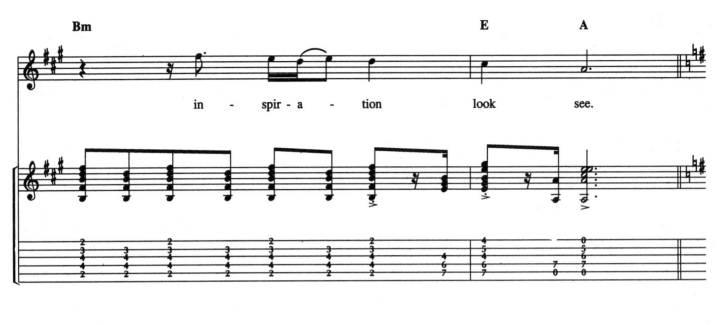

in - spir - a - tion   look   see.

Electric 12 string Guitar

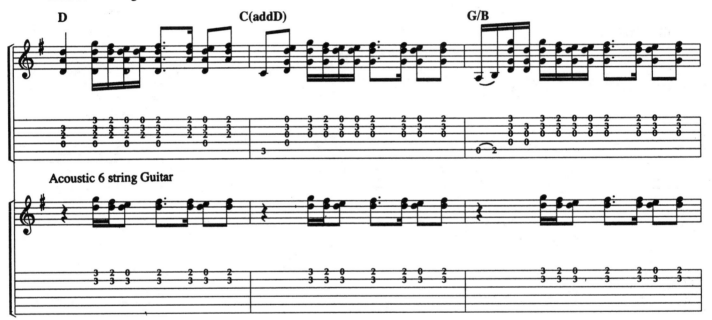

Acoustic 6 string Guitar

Rhythm Figure 1 (Electric 12 string Guitar only)

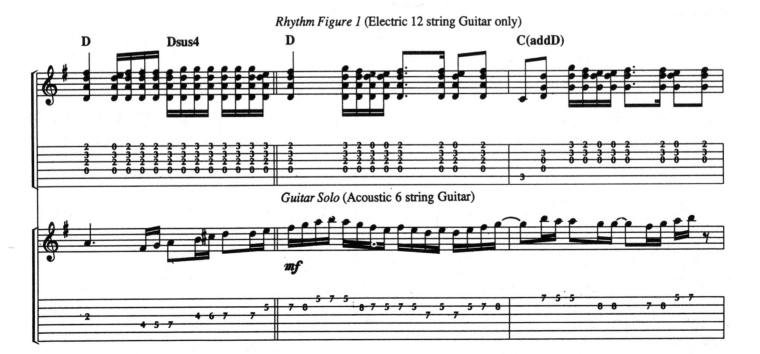

Guitar Solo (Acoustic 6 string Guitar)

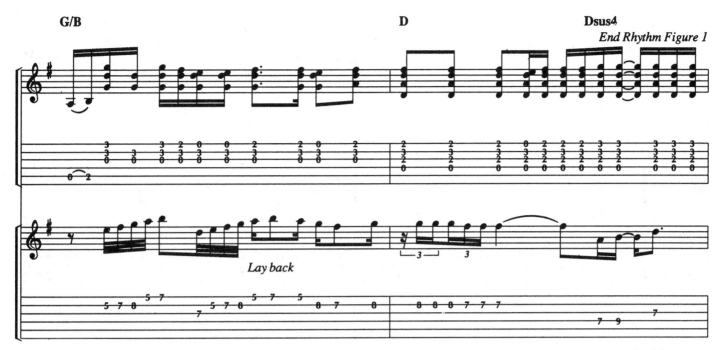

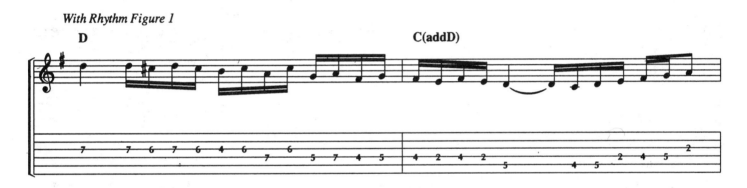

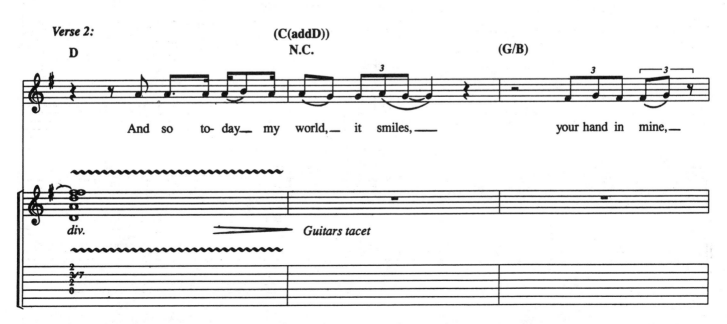

And so to-day my world, it smiles, your hand in mine,

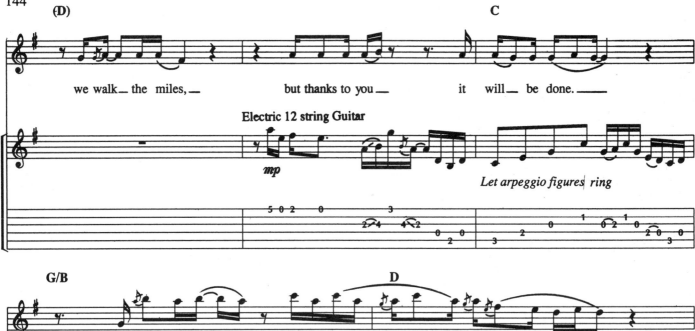

we walk_ the miles,_ but thanks to you _ it will_ be done._

Electric 12 string Guitar

mp

Let arpeggio figures ring

For you to me _____ are the on - ly one. _____

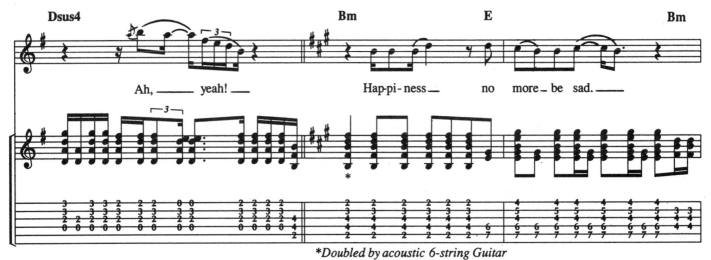

Ah, _____ yeah! _ Hap-pi-ness_ no more_ be sad. _

*Doubled by acoustic 6-string Guitar

Verse 3:

Hap-pi- ness_____ I'm_ glad. If the sun re-

Guitars tacet

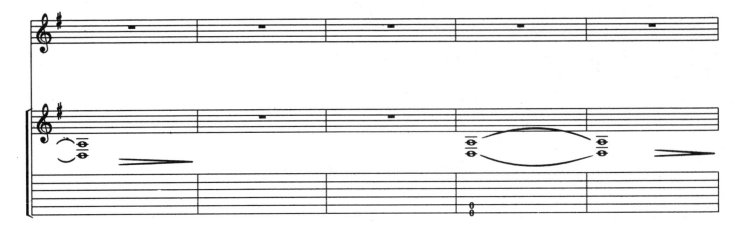

(C)
N.C. **(G/B)** **D5** **(C)**
N.C.

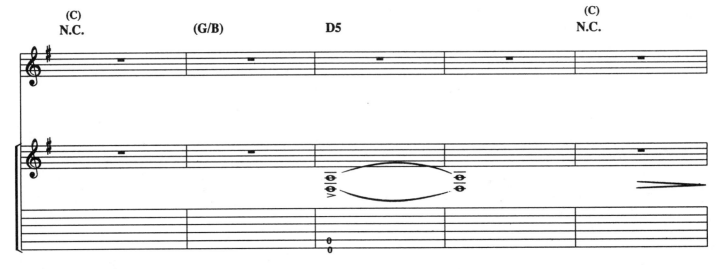

(G/B) **D5**

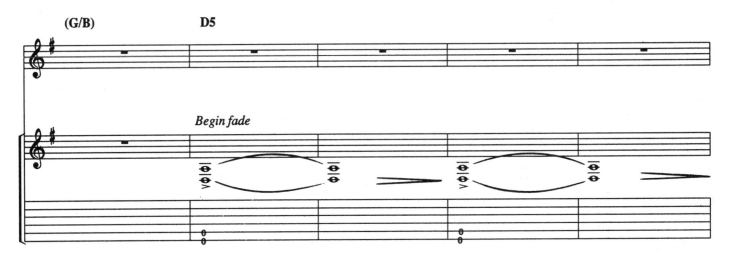

Begin fade

Fade out

Fade out *Fade in*

ppp *mp* *f*

Most guitarists have — or want to have — one foot in the traditional scene and one foot in the contemporary scene. This method addresses both styles with charismatic flair AND solid pedagogy.

Most teachers want to teach according to the needs of individual students. With all the options in Belwin's 21st Century Guitar Library, teachers have it all!

classical ■ rock ■ pop ■ folk
lead guitar ■ rock rhythm
standard notation and tablature
accompaniments
blues and rock riffs ■ power chords
lead scales
note reading ■ creativity
lesson plans ■ performance tips
fretboard understanding
musicianship

Available from your favorite music dealer:

LEVEL 1
(EL 03842) Guitar Method 1
(EL 03842AT) Guitar Method 1 w/Cassette
(EL 03842CD) Guitar Method 1 w/CD
(EL 03851AT) Guitar Rock Shop 1 w/Cassette
(EL 03851CD) Guitar Rock Shop 1 w/CD
(EL 03845) Guitar Theory 1
(EL 03848AT) Guitar Song Trax 1 w/Cassette
(EL 03848CD) Guitar Song Trax 1 w/CD
(EL 03955S) Guitar Ensemble Student Book 1
(EL 03955AT) Guitar Ensemble Score Book 1
    w/Cassette
(EL 03955CD) Guitar Ensemble Score Book 1
    w/CD
(EL 03960) Guitar Teacher Edition 1

LEVEL 2
(EL 03843) Guitar Method 2
(EL 03843AT) Guitar Method 2 w/Cassette
(EL 03843CD) Guitar Method 2 w/CD
(EL 03852AT) Guitar Rock Shop 2 w/Cassette
(EL 03852CD) Guitar Rock Shop 2 w/CD
(EL 03846) Guitar Theory 2
(EL 03849AT) Guitar Song Trax 2 w/Cassette
(EL 03849CD) Guitar Song Trax 2 w/CD
(EL 03957S) Guitar Ensemble Student Book 2
(EL 03957AT) Guitar Ensemble Score Book 2
    w/Cassette
(EL 03957CD) Guitar Ensemble Score Book 2
    w/CD
(EL 03961) Guitar Teacher Edition 2

Level 3 coming soon

INTRODUCING

Belwin's 21st Century Guitar Library